Stuck
in a
Sticky
World

Stuck
in a
Sticky
World

Learning to See God's
Best in Life's Worst

JON JOHNSTON

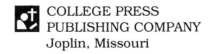
COLLEGE PRESS
PUBLISHING COMPANY
Joplin, Missouri

Library of Congress Cataloging-in-Publication Data

Johnston, Jon.
   Stuck in a sticky world: learning to see God's best in
life's worst / Jon Johnston.
     p. cm.
   Includes bibliographical references.
   ISBN 0-89900-752-X
   1. Christian life. 2. Interpersonal relations—
Religious aspects—Christianity. I. Title.
BV4509.5J6457 1996
248.4—dc20   96-1631
                                        CIP

Dedicated to

PEPPERDINE UNIVERSITY

my home for
two fulfilling decades

where
natural beauty is inviting
colleagues are inspiring
students are challenging
standards are demanding
and
values are Christian

In Memoriam to
three very good friends:

MICHAEL ANDERSON
(1942-1993)

CARL GAEDE
(1936-1995)

CLAUDE KENNEDY
(1920-1995)

Table of Contents

APPENDIXES

Foreword

In my experience, I have found that when a person is "stuck" in a desperate situation — when even well-meaning friends, professional counselors and a host of "how to" books offer no satisfactory solutions — the powerful love of our Lord provides the answer.

Following the death of my nineteen-year-old daughter, Diane, I spent much of the next twenty years in the crusade against drug abuse. My "education" took me from the inner city ghetto to the finest psychiatrists, social workers, and drug counselors in the world.

I researched every known method of fighting drug addiction. I went on drug raids with "narcs," sat in on dramatic confrontations at "free clinics," consoled bereaved parents, and had my heart broken by kids who fell back into drugs and died.

I never saw a permanent "cure" unless God came into the life of the addict. I never saw anyone come "unstuck" in life's worst swamp unless it was accompanied by the inner change that only the love of Jesus can effect.

That's why we need this book to reach into the lives of unhappy people who find themselves unable to dig out from life's morass.

As a member of the Board of Regents of Pepperdine University I want to thank Dr. Jon Johnston for dedicating this book to our Christian educational mission.

As a member of the troubled human race, I pray for its success.

Art Linkletter

Introduction

It was a fall weekend during my Junior year of high school. The air was crisp, leaves were a riot of color, and snow-capped mountains enhanced the southern California skyline.

A couple of buddies and I jumped into our family car (which dad loaned reluctantly), and headed for Big Bear Lake. We planned to snag a bushel of sweet-tasting, mountain trout.

Our departure was late, and we arrived in darkness — during a blizzard. Land and lake were frozen solid. With the wisdom of a gnat, I decided to drive off-road, and park along the water's edge.

Out came the equipment. After rigging-up, we walked along the shore, casting, getting tangled, teasing, laughing. Any fish in our vicinity, no doubt, raced away to avoid our chatter and clatter.

Gradually, the golden sun began to "chin itself" on the eastern horizon. Its warmth was soothing, and its light permitted us to see our surroundings.

I glanced toward our car, and suddenly gulped. Something was dreadfully wrong. The shoreline had thawed, and the vehicle's tires were completely submerged in the mud. Next to go would be the entire "Body by Fisher."

In panic, we tossed aside our gear, made a rapid beeline to town, and found a tow truck driver with a very long cable. Tugging feverishly for an hour, from 100 feet away, he succeeded in pulling our car from its sinking pit. Then, he gleefully charged us an arm and a leg.

Although we left financially obliterated, fishless, and in a car that looked like it had just raced in a mud derby, we were greatly relieved. We had been thoroughly stuck, but now we were free!

Have you ever been stuck? Bogged-down in a situation that seemed inescapable? Unresolvable? Even incomprehensible? If so, welcome to the human race — and to this book's pages.

It's referred to with many down-home expressions, among them:

- ✧ cornered   ✧ beached   ✧ hemmed-in
- ✧ logjammed   ✧ shot down   ✧ tanked
- ✧ up the creek   ✧ in a pickle   ✧ pinned to the mat

There are an incredible number of ways to get stuck. Freeway jam-ups. Phone calls, especially from telemarketers. Computer glitches. Inclement weather. Detours.

Then, there are those times when we just *feel* stuck. When Cherry and I attend an event at our local Civic Arts Theatre, we feel imprisoned. With few exits and no left aisle, in case of fire, we'd probably be "toast."

All of these physical entrapments make us frustrated — especially if we're a "Type A Personality" (i.e., impatient, tense, wired).

But, this book highlights a kind of stuckness that's even more excruciating. One involving relationships with "impossible people." Impasses that remain, in spite of our best efforts and noblest intentions.

Our teenagers refuse to shape up. The minister accuses of us being neglectful toward a relative in the hospital, just because we don't happen to be there when he visits. The spouse we cherish remains mistrusting. Just when we thought our boss couldn't get worse, he becomes an "overachiever."

We're stuck. We know self-help books by heart. We've prayed for hours. We've done all we know to "make things right." Result: The same as if I had jumped into that sinking car, and began racing the engine — rapidly spinning wheels and going nowhere!

The truth faces us squarely: Relationship blockages can make us feel as "locked-in" as any life-termer in the penitentiary. Solutions appear distant; misery weighs heavily; hope seems gone. Our self-confidence plummets, and, worst of all, we even become less sure of God.

This book proposes a fresh approach to such dilemmas. One that is certain to get us back on track. Unstuck. Free and moving forward.

It all comes down to our **perspective**. How we envision the circumstances and people in the drama of our life story. And, how we "see" that we are being seen — and how that affects our thoughts and feelings.

In a nutshell, we must see things from a biblical perspective. This involves reframing life's "picture," so that it has a different look — and we have a new outlook. One that is generated from a pure heart.

Paul (Eph. 1:18) prays that "the eyes of our hearts" might be enlightened. What does that mean? Is there really such a thing as spiritual insight? If so, what is its source, and how is it "channeled" to us? What are its dramatic effects on our lives?

To the courageous and sincere, God offers a warm invitation to improved vision. Vision that looks beyond the present. Beyond the negative. Beyond the human. Vision that frees us from life's sinkholes!

Furthermore, unlike that tow truck fellow, our heavenly Father won't charge a dime!

I wish to offer special thanks to four special persons, whose ideas greatly assisted me in this project: Pam Campbell, Steve Green, Norman Shoemaker, and LaGard Smith.

Getting Stuck

CHAPTER ONE

Anybody See an Exit?

"Yet man is born to trouble as surely as sparks fly upward."
(Job 5:7)
*"Pain is God's megaphone. He whispers to us
in our pleasure, but shouts to us in our pain."*
(C.S. Lewis)
"In life . . . the turkeys always seem to outnumber the eagles."
(Charles R. Swindoll)

As a kid, I put church leaders up there with baseball heroes and chocolate Hershey kisses. Why? My
dad was one, and he was the most gentle and humble
man I have ever known.

Was I a tad idealistic? You bet. Still am — even
after all the pain. Let me explain. I was mistreated.
My assailant was a church leader. And, neither of us
was affiliated with any cult.[1] It all happened in a typical church setting.

---

1. Cf. Ronald M. Enroth, *Churches That Abuse: Help for
Those Hurt by Legalism, Authoritarian Leadership, Manipu-
lation, Excessive Discipline, Spiritual Intimidation* (Grand
Rapids: Zondervan, 1992).

This author focuses upon abuses, and their effects, that
emerge in extremely repressive religious environments. Ones
that feature near-total control by authoritarian leaders, with

Today, I'm only able to talk about it because of the peace that has come through forgiveness. I honestly wish my assailant God's best. But, back to my story.

It began like a honeymoon. Very quickly, this guy captured my respect and fit my childhood ideal to a "T." I just knew we would work harmoniously together, and more important, deepen spiritually!

Furthermore, I was confident that the feeling was mutual. He asked me to serve on his leadership team. Our relationship seemed (and was) absolutely ideal — that is, until. . . .

Zippo, with about as much warning as a California Angels losing streak, things turned ugly. And to this day, I'm clueless as to what instigated the change.

The fellow turned suspicious and unaccepting. Somewhere, somehow, he bought into a fictitious message — *Jon Johnston is trying to do you in, and is influencing others to join him.*

This leader seemed driven to believe this misinformation, form misjudgments, and engage in mistreatment. Toward myself, and those whom I had, supposedly, convinced to dislike him.

Predictably, it wasn't long before many of the "targeted" resigned from their leadership positions. I, masochistically, retained my seat on the board, and

---

constant intimidation and threats for anyone veering from the strict, narrow pathway.

Although this is an accurate, well-researched, and needed resource for our society, another book should be written on the kinds of abuse that take place in more normal religious settings. Abuse that occurs, for example, when power-games are played by leaders to manipulate followers. When not-so-subtle pressures are exerted on parishioners to be loyal, unquestioning, sacrificial, etc.

continued to teach my adult Sunday School class.

Nagging fears and questions began to swirl in my brain. Nothing, even remotely like this, had ever happened. Why now? Why was this church leader stomping on my childhood ideal? On my credibility? On our relationship?

Groping For Answers

Before long, I started second-guessing. Perhaps, this was all a figment of my imagination. It wasn't really happening.

Or, maybe, it was a brief phase allowed by God to build character, or teach valuable lessons. But, wouldn't He desire that His "sheep" be protected from assault? Even more important, doesn't He expect His leaders to live exemplary lives — uplifting and affirming, rather than tearing down those to whom they minister?

In desperation, I began to air-express "SOS" prayers, and encouraged friends to do likewise.

One day, with perplexed mind and aching heart, I calmly approached this leader to ask "why?" I honestly say that I only desired reconciliation, resolution, restoration.

His response wasn't warm. All attempts to clarify motives were seen as schemes to hide and twist the truth. Furthermore, he seemed to imply that all bridges between us were irreparable.

We had other meetings — some even included mediators. Things only got worse. My frustration soared; the hurt became unbearable. Every night, I prayed myself to sleep.

My deep desire was to quit and avoid further hurt. Didn't Jesus instruct His disciples to *"shake the dust from their shoes,*" (i.e., depart, never to return, see Matt. 10:14), as a response to this kind of rejection?

But, there were three good reasons for hanging tough: 1) My nemesis might "see the light" and change his viewpoint. 2) I felt a compassion for, and a desire to protect, the others being assaulted. 3) God had not issued me an "exit visa." For His reasons, He wanted me to stay put.

Intellectually, I bought into these — but emotionally, it was another story. No need to deny it. I was thoroughly stuck!

Goodbye Rainstorm, Hello Typhoon!

One day, a board member requested that I contact a man about serving as treasurer. His request seemed simple and reasonable.

I complied, and asked the fellow to get back to me with his answer. My reasoning went: if he declines, nothing need be said — a closed issue; if he accepts, my friend can pass along the information to the church leader.

Logical? I certainly thought so. Innocent? Absolutely.

But, suddenly it became "fodder for the accusation mill." The fellow I approached, unfortunately, had already bought into the leader's suspicions. He quickly phoned him with "evidence of my attempt to undercut his authority." Strike three!

I was summoned to meet with the board, some of whom had been prepped to buy into the accusation. Although no kangaroos were present when we met, it was their kind of court session — if you catch my drift.

If only it were a joke, or even a nightmare — but it was sheer reality.

My friends defended me for awhile. But then, one by one, they resigned and stormed out in disgust — leaving me to face my "inquisition" alone. Innuendos, insinuations, and suspicions were voiced.

Before long, consensus was reached by those who remained: "Jon is a trouble-causing power-monger who lies to appear innocent." One demanded that I resign; others relished the thought of "kicking me out."

How should I respond? My thoughts focused on what my dear, servant father might advise. His style was always to "go that extra mile in love."

I suggested that I might sign a statement pledging loyalty.

Without admitting to any guilt, I would assure leader and board of my support — and be assured of theirs. This gesture would quell remaining suspicions, recast me as "on the team," and put the whole matter to rest once and for all. The board went for it, or so it seemed.

We agreed that the signed statement would be held in strictest confidence.

Once again, I was clobbered by my naive idealism, for I underestimated the intent of my accusers! Far from being finished, they used the paper as "an admission of guilt" — a weapon for further accusation.

Furthermore, the confidentiality they promised was totally breached! It spread everywhere, with the credibility of a tabloid.

In good faith, I had agreed to be totally supportive — believing that the leader would reciprocate. But, by doing this, I was "hung out to dry" when he promptly continued with his old tricks.

His cronies decided to refrain from speaking to me. Also, to turn their backs whenever I approached. Didn't they do that to Aaron Burr?

In desperation, the only thing I could think to do was try harder. Do more. Prove that I wasn't an ogre. So, I volunteered to take on more responsibilities. My overtures were spurned.

The pain began to get unbearable, and adversely affect my normal functioning. My behavior. My attitude. Sensing that I had run out of all options, I quietly departed. Dejected. Disillusioned. Wiped out.

But, that was then. This is now. Joyfully, I declare that I'm no longer stuck. I've emerged from that deep sinkhole, and stand firmly on solid ground. Jesus has brought freedom. And, as a bonus, some great lessons.

How did this change occur? What lessons were learned? My answers to these questions will be shared, in bits and pieces, throughout the book.

I warmly invite you to accompany me on this reflective journey. To begin, let's lean in a bit closer to focus on nagging, relationship dilemmas. The kind most all of us, undoubtedly, have found to be stubbornly inescapable and unresolvable.

Lone Rangers We're Not!

Some of life's ditches are conducive to rather quick solutions. In football, with a fourth-down-and-long-yardage situation, we punt. At a rodeo, when a raging bull starts to stomp the cowboy he just bucked off, we send in the clown. When our pipes get clogged, we call the plumber.

But relationship impasses are a "horse of another color." They're much more complex, and difficult to cope with. Why? Because they involve the wills of others.

Put simply, resolution requires that wills converge, if not in agreement, at least in cooperation. The old adage holds true: *it takes (at least) two persons to have a good relationship, but only one is needed to ruin it.*

Realizing this brought little encouragement to me. In fact, it intensified my self-pity. My assailant wasn't about to suddenly will me anything but misery!

Then something dawned on me: I wasn't "The Lone Ranger." Relationship stuckness is a basic fact of all of us — whether rich or poor, powerful or weak, attractive or beastly. We're all destined to slide into one or more of these horrible ditches.

And it has always been that way.

In the mood for a bit of History 101? Even a cursory recall of yesterday's stalwarts brings to mind their grappling with sticky interpersonal predicaments.

- **Socrates**, charged with corrupting the minds of Athenian youth, ended up guzzling hemlock;
- **Mahatma Gandhi** reached an impasse with the Brits, and nearly starved himself to death to make his point;
- **Abe Lincoln** accepted the blame for his marital strife, and acknowledged that his political enemies dogged his every move.
- **Ronald and Nancy Reagan** continuously grieved over the extremely strained relationships they had with her daughter, Patti.

Likewise, many of our favorite biblical personalities were no prima donnas when it came to relationship dead ends. In the Old Testament recall:

> **Cain's** "sibling rivalry" with Abel resulted in the world's first homicide. The same sickness afflicted the brothers of Joseph, and the "elder brother" of the Prodigal Son.

> **David's** bad chemistry with Saul is familiar to us, as was his grief-stricken relationship with his son, Absalom.

> **Elijah's** intense feud with Jezebel caused him to run, then hide under a Juniper tree — and blabber annihilistic self-talk.

> **Daniel's** run-in with jealous Persian politicians nearly resulted in his becoming "Alpo for Lions."

Are New Testament heroes immune? Consider:

> **Paul's** verbal "duking-out" with Demetrius the Silversmith in Ephesus. The latter's idol business "tanked" when the Apostle convinced scores to trash their images and turn to the true God.

> **James and John's** soured relationship with the other disciples, after they had blatantly engaged in one-upmanship — requesting Jesus to make them "top dogs" in His eternal kingdom.

> **Peter's** strained relationship with new Gentile Christians, which only improved after Paul berated his chauvinism.

> **Jesus'** tons of skirmishes and impasses, with:
> Pharisees,
> brothers,
> hometown folks (Nazarenes),
> swine ranchers — who objected to their pigs' aquatics,

Judas, and (for that matter),
the remainder of the disciples, who
never really grasped His message
until after His death and resurrection

Spits, Skewers and Slow Burns

When I think about the penchant for stuckness, I
can't help envisioning a barbecue rotisserie. A long
sharp prong is inserted into a piece of meat, and it
slowly turns as it sizzles. Appropriate imagery for
some of our predicaments!

It's certainly no picnic for us to be stuck. Especially when:

> ➤ we're not at fault, unlike the person who brings
> the wrath of the law upon himself by robbing a
> bank;
> ➤ we've done all we know to get free — reason,
> talk, manipulate, read, pray — but to no avail;
> ➤ we're certain it might have all been prevented,
> through recognizing danger signals, seeking
> advice, etc.

The story I've shared betrays my intense repul-
sion of relationship impasses. I can think of no worse
kind. When:

. . . relationships go sour
. . . bad words and worse feelings emerge;
. . . "interested bystanders" become aware,
and begin forming distorted judgments.

There are many instances of such "crunch situations":

> ➤ aged parents, though dependent, becoming
> stubborn toward children seeking their welfare;
> ➤ bosses abusing, with threat and intimidation;

> co-workers manipulating and deceiving, to get ahead;
> spouses pursuing pathways of infidelity;
> teens refusing to take responsibility for their actions.

Again, who could deny: We're quick to feel the impact, and resulting pain, of relationship dilemmas. All too often the hurt does not disappear, or even subside — even after doing our very best to rectify and reconcile.

Such impasses cause intense, deeply-penetrating discomfort and confusion. So much so that we're tempted to conclude: There is, simply, no way out.

Got a Moment?

Pause with me, just long enough to reflect on a few questions. They're not meant to cause discomfort. Please respond as honestly as you possibly can.

Begin by thinking of a time when you found yourself in an unresolvable dilemma. Stuck.

1. **How did it feel? (Like an exciting challenge? A punishment from God? A statement about my self-worth? Just another part of life?)**

2. **Whom did I tell about it, and why? (Jesus? Best friend(s)? Nobody?)**

3. **How did I respond? (Confrontationally? Passively — holding it all in? Pretending it wasn't there?)**

4. What "toll" did it take on me? (On me — in terms of behavior, confidence, faith? On those closest to me? On others?)

5. What thoughts did I have that were the most helpful? What actions did I take that greatly assisted me?

6. Am I satisfied with how I responded? Why or why not? If not, how might I have responded differently?

One final question: Am I open to considering (and possibly trying) a new approach? If so, please continue with me on our journey.

It's time to focus on just how we might have gotten stuck. What's more, how we remained that way. In the next chapter we'll examine possible reasons, in hopes of avoiding that trap again — once we're free.

CHAPTER TWO

When Push Turns to Shove

"Traumatic experiences leave me in a quandary: I hurt too bad to laugh, and I'm too big to cry."
(Lyndon Baines Johnson)

"You don't walk close to God for very long before you become the face on someone's dartboard."
(Charles Swindoll)

"The cheese tastes great, but this trap is a real nuisance!"
(The Proverbial Mouse)

Tokyo, at rush hour, is one wild, gigantic crush — very similar to what occurs in a trash compacter. In this environment, even a sardine would get a raging case of claustrophobia!

Throngs push and squeeze to jam on the subways. But here's the real kicker: designated "pushers" (ungently) shove people on board. And, surprisingly, passengers don't seem to get ticked-off at these aggressive manhandlers. In fact, they appear somewhat grateful.

Such a practice would incite skirmishes, perhaps even riots, in our country. We demand privacy and freedom — and that means giving us our space.[1] Few

---

1. Social psychologists refer to *"reactance,"* when explaining

things infuriate us more than being shoved — anytime, for any reason. Especially, if we're pushed in a direction we don't wish to go.

The first chapter declares that, at times, we all get stuck in relationships. It seems like some people in our lives are covered with Velcro or tar, prepared to hold us fast if we get too close.

Admittedly, sometimes we're the varmint. We stumble into impasses by becoming lazy, aggressive, vindictive, aloof, stubborn or naive. In such instances, we earn and own the greatest share of any blame.

But this book focuses on how circumstances, beyond our control, often push us into getting stuck. We haven't brought it on ourselves. And, goodness knows, it's the last thing we'd ever wish for. But, nevertheless, the nagging truth remains — STUCK R US!

What are these unfortunate, intruding circumstances that sucker us into interpersonal roadblocks? Let's lean in to examine some:

A favorite author of mine, and seminary professor, Lewis B. Smedes, describes four of these culprits.

> We are stuck with the *genes* we neither earned
> nor asked for. We are sucked into (role) *games.*

---

how Americans respond to feeling pushed into something. It is defined as "a disagreeable emotional and cognitive reaction to the restriction of one's freedom." It causes people to feel hostility and anger, and as a result, to seek to restore their freedom. Ironically, reactance often motivates people to pursue the restricted behavior with renewed vigor, e.g., go against their doctor's orders when they feel he has been too restrictive. (Robert S. Feldman, *Social Psychology*. Englewood Cliffs, NJ: Prentice-Hall, 1995), p. 170.

... We are walloped by private *tragedies*. ... And we all rise and fall with the American *dollar*."[2]

Let's briefly unpack each of these guys: genes, game-playing, tragedies and bucks.

Genes: Nature's Circuitboard

We're all born with unique genetic characteristics that chart our course. Some predispose us to strengths: long life, Paul Newman-like eyes, genius minds, immunity against disease. Others push us toward deficiencies: color-blindness, baldness, retardation.

In addition to these tendencies related to our physical natures, we are scripted toward certain psychological temperaments. Gary Smalley and John Trent's popular book, *The Two Sides of Love,* presents a delightful typology — likening our human temperaments to animal characteristics.[3] Let's pause to have a look at these, and attempt to pinpoint which one (or more) we most resemble. It will be fun.

---

2. Lewis B. Smedes, *Caring and Commitment: Learning to Live the Love We Promise* (San Francisco: Harper and Row, Publishers, 1988), p. 148.

3. Gary Smalley and John Trent, Ph.D., *The Two Sides of Love: What Strengthens Affection, Closeness and Lasting Commitment.* (Pomona, CA: Focus on the Family Publishing. Copyright © 1990, 1992. Used by permission of Focus on the Family.) The typology is presented in chapters four through seven.

Rather than appealing to us to attempt to abandon our basic temperament — something they consider impossible — the authors admonish us to strive for Christlike balance, and to "file off the rough edges."

Also, to develop a deep appreciation for different temperaments in others. (A study of 200 very fulfilled Swedish couples was cited. Their most prevailing characteristic? They learned to value their partners' differences.)

LION
✧ ideal roles: leader, entrepreneur
✧ characteristics: decisive, take-charge, assertive, bold, goal-driven, enterprising, decision-maker, (favorite saying: *"Let's go for it!"*)
✧ time frame: the immediate present (want things now)
✧ lessons he/she needs to learn:
   1) Questions are healthy — patiently listen to suggestions or answers;
   2) Chit-chat, without immediate problem solution, is valuable;
   3) Projects aren't as important as people.

OTTER
✧ ideal roles: motivator, encourager
✧ characteristics: "parties-waiting-to-happen," fun-loving, verbal, creative, mixes easily, enjoys change, avoids details, group-oriented, impulsive, often late without remorse, optimistic (favorite sayings: *"Lighten up"* and *"Just trust me."*)
✧ time frame: future (put-off, procrastinate)
✧ lessons he/she needs to learn:
   1) Having fun has its consequences — not all good;
   2) Deadlines aren't the same as guidelines;
   3) He/she is the most susceptible to peer pressure, group-think, conformity.

GOLDEN RETRIEVER
✧ ideal roles: counselor, servant
✧ characteristics: loyal, even-keeled, enjoys routine, good listener, nurturer, sympathetic, tolerant, adaptable, sensitive (e.g., buys 10 boxes of Girls Scout cookies), (favorite saying: *"Tell me absolutely everything."*)
✧ time frame: present (attentive to others' needs immediately)

✧ lessons he/she needs to learn:
   1) Learn to say "no" when necessary (set guide-lines);
   2) He/she is the most susceptible to codependent relationships, or, carrying all the problems on his/her shoulders;
   3) There is a need to make decisions (i.e., be assertive), even though there is a risk some-one may be hurt.

BEAVER
✧ ideal roles: artist, engineer
✧ characteristics: perfectionist, deliberate, factual, detailed, reserved, practical (even boring), "God's architect," thinks in columns, reads instruction books, precise, persistent (favorite saying: *"Let's do it right."*)
✧ time frame: past (prides himself/herself in track record)
✧ lessons he/she needs to learn:
   1) Have patience with imperfect people and their imperfections.
   2) Understand the need for trade-offs. (With some of life's demands, we can't spend inordi-nate amounts of energy, time, and money to "do it right.")
   3) Be gentle. (Because he/she can take things apart so well, the temptation is to do the same with people).

It should be noted that the lion and beaver tend to be *"hardsided"* (harsh, cold), while the otter and golden retriever lean toward being *"softsided"* (toler-ant, warm).

Being too much of either can cause us to get stuck in relationships. Excessive hardness can lead to aggression and insensitivity; a ton of softness can yield vulnerability and indecision.

More specifically, each "animal" has definite tendencies that can lead to relationship logjams. For example, a lion has a strong propensity toward impatience — while a golden retriever can easily slip into the ditch of codependency. (Refer to "lessons he/she needs to learn" under each "animal" discussed.)

Note: After picking the animal(s) we think we most resemble, we can take the "animal test." It is very brief, and is located in Appendix A. Also, in this same Appendix is an exercise which reveals how "hardsided" or "softsided" we are. Results are great for discussion or for personal, prayerful introspection.

The Script Society Shoves Into Our Hand

In addition to being pushed by our unique temperamental propensities, we're driven by roles our world forces upon us.[4]

In our technologically sophisticated age, we feel insignificant — unloved for who we are. This notion is reinforced by our impersonal world. Result: We conclude that our only value lies in the scripted collection of roles we're made to play. Lars Wilhelmsson says:[5]

To the doctor — I'm a patient
To the politician — a constituent
To the lawyer — a client

---

4. The standard definition of *"role"* is: "how you respond, behaviorally and attitudinally, to your position in any/all of the five societal institutions (education, family, religion, economy, government)." For example, related to the family institution, your role is the manner in which you respond to your position as husband, daughter, etc.

5. Lars Wilhelmsson, *Making Forever Friends* (Torrance, CA: Martin Press, 1982), pp. 112-113.

To the retailer — a shopper
To the editor — a subscriber
To the sports promoter — a fan
To the minister — a parishioner
To the educator — a student
To the military — a soldier/number
To the banker — a depositor/borrower
To the manufacturer — a salesman
To the airlines — a passenger

Because we're role-labeled, we feel pushed to fulfill role obligations. Sociologists agree that our roles mold us more than we influence our roles. In essence, we become our roles.

We take on role uniforms, political attitudes, lifestyles and products. When we, for example, come into contact with musicians, construction workers or accountants, we realize that each has an "identity package." It's a good bet that musicians will refrain from wearing construction work site attire to performances, and homebuilders will not hold memberships in the A.C.L.U.!

How does role-playing push us into relationship impasses? Very simply, we can experience difficulty in authentically relating to persons of other roles. How long has it been since you were "snowed" with role jargon? (Spoken to your doctor lately? How about your computer repairman or lawyer?) Words used, and positions defended, predictably align with our role positions. In a sense, our roles often blind us.

Some scholars I've known come across as stilted and unapproachable. They take on a role disguise that makes them sound and appear omniscient and authoritative.

This fictitious image, intended to command respect, often blocks natural, affirming relationships. The kind necessary for real rapport.

The same can be said for all of us who allow our role-tag to submerge our personhood. Our relationships are bound to reach communication impasses. One of the surest indications of being thoroughly stuck!

Tragedy: Life's Unwelcome Interruption

How many times have we heard sentences that start: "Everything was going so great, but then it all ended when _____"? The pressures, associated with adverse circumstances, can result in all sorts of relationship blockages.

One sad response is abandonment. Recently I heard that 52% of husbands whose wives contract multiple sclerosis (the disease of women in their 30s) "hit the road." The traumatic thoughts of caring for an invalid, and watching her deteriorate, prompt them to head for the exit. Obviously, the abandoned remain stuck — deeply grieved, uncared for, desperate. And for absolutely no fault of their own.

Just as anguishing are the "blame-attacks," frequently waged after a child is born with deficiencies. Both partners conclude that they are stuck for the long haul. No escape routes in sight. It's then that directing accusations toward the other spouse becomes a frequent, counterproductive attempt to assuage the deep hurt. Unfortunately, the opposite occurs.

Why does tragedy push us into relational impasses? Much of it has to do with the nature of our grieving. In processing such loss, according to

Kübler-Ross (*On Death And Dying*), we typically touch base with these stages: denial, anger/rage, bargaining (with God), depression — then, hopefully, acceptance.[6]

This is a bumpy road for us to travel, accompanied by a kaleidoscope of emotions. Often, persons near us become the targets of our extreme distress. With a negatively-distorted view of reality — seeing it as dark, ugly and threatening — we're apt to envision persons nearby as culpable and offensive.

Thank goodness, this need not occur. Furthermore, if it does, it need not persist.

Can tragedies push us to the brink of becoming stuck in relationships? The answer is evident.

The Dollar Crunch

Financial demands can also put a real crimp in relationships. When suddenly locked into a necessity to obtain cash, we often panic. The situation becomes ripe for "finger-pointing," intense competition and skyrocketing levels of stress.

Our options are clear. Either it's cut-back-and-do-without — reducing the perceived quality of life. Or, we're impelled to take on additional employment to close the gap. In either case, exhaustion and interpersonal conflict are likely to occur.

We can get stuck with financial hardship, and it can wear us down. Added pressures prompt us to be "on edge." In addition, we have little time, energy and money to invest in those we love.

When it comes to our relationships, it's a clear case of high demand and low investment. Our "love

---

6. Elisabeth Kübler-Ross, *On Death And Dying* (New York: Macmillan, 1969).

bank" can go bankrupt. Why? Few deposits.

Little about poverty is enticing or endearing. As a rule, financial need extracts a very heavy toll. It pushes, and often tears apart relationships. Parents and their children often feel entrapped. We hear despondent comments like:

"It doesn't seem like we'll ever get our heads above water."

"What could we ever have done to deserve this?"

"Our happiness flew right out the door, when our financial resources went dry."

Could anyone deny the "push potential" of extreme financial shortfall? Unless wise, persistent measures are taken, relationships can rapidly deteriorate.

Allow me to add a couple more pushers to Smedes' list.

Group-think or Else!

We hear: "If you're *really* loyal to our _____ (church, minister, family, friends, job, ethnic group, nation, etc.) you'll _____" (take this stand, do this, think this way, etc.).

It's a basic axiom in sociology: All social groups, with whom we identify and receive support, demand our conformity. We're asked to "run up their flag" on our personal flagpole — to adopt "group-think."

To renege, express distaste, or even hesitate is to be tagged a "deviant" — along with all the ostracism, denial, and punishment thereto appertaining. So, all too often, we go along to get along.

Unfortunately, this frequently lands us squarely in a ditch. Why? Because we can go against our personal beliefs and desires. For example, consider:

➤ scores who have married "the family choice," in spite of deep personal misgivings, and therefore reaped a life of regret;

➤ multitudes who have, unsatisfyingly, followed their father's occupational footsteps;

➤ throngs who have, with deep misgivings, continued abiding by the "family religion" — realizing that exploring other beliefs would result in reprimand or harsh rejection. (*example:* In Israel, orthodox Jews conduct "funerals," symbolizing disownment, for any family member who converts to Christianity.)

If only, as David Reisman declares, people could be *"inner-directed"* rather than either *"tradition-directed"* (taking cues from the past) or *"other-directed"* (being driven by others' opinions). If only people would be guided by inner conviction, objectivity and principle.[7]

Then, perhaps, relationships that result would be less likely to self-destruct. To gravitate toward resentment and counterproductive living.

Allow me to mention one last circumstance that pushes us. One that could be the most powerful, and exasperating of all. One that sneaks up on us like a skillful bandit.

The Desensitizing Nature of Relationships

Our heart and mind team up to land us into relationship traps. Usually, this occurs over a period of time. Things just gradually worsen while we, for

---

7. David Reisman, *The Lonely Crowd: A Study of the Changing American Character* (New Haven, CT: Yale University Press, 1970, originally 1950).

whatever reason(s), do nothing. Social psychologists refer to this as *"psychic numbing."*[8]

A helpful way to envision this phenomenon is provided by Charles Bolton — who equates relationships with escalator rides. His primary focus is romantic pairing, but his principle is applicable to all kinds of people-bonding.

To paraphrase Bolton: All we need to do is take the first step, stay on, and the other steps take themselves. We're heading for a destination — like it or not. And the closer we get, the more difficult it is to jump off.

He adds this caveat. Whenever we become involved with another, we actually ride on five escalators at once! This makes reversing ourselves that many times more difficult.

What are Bolton's *"relationship escalators?"*[9]

1. **idealization**: We inflate the other's attributes in our mind, and derive great ego-satisfaction from being paired with the "wonderperson" our mind has created.

2. **fantasy**: We create a "Camelot relationship" with the person, which is difficult to relinquish.

3. **involvement**: Our habit patterns become bound, and interdependent, with the other person's. Result: To experience something without him/her is a downer.

---

8. The term, *"psychic numbing"* refers to "an emotional self-anesthesia" that often occurs in relationships. Those involved become unreflective and unresponsive — in spite of evidences of deterioration and/or discomfort. There is an absence of intentional effort to grow or change.(Charles R. Swindoll, *The Quest for Character* (Portland, OR: Multnomah Press, 1987).

9. Charles Bolton, source unpublished or unknown.

4. **addiction**: Increasingly, we become unwilling to go through "withdrawal pains" of giving him/her up — even though we know it is wise to do.

5. **commitment**: After being tagged a "couple," having exchanged tokens of affection, etc. others demand that we stay together.

Admittedly, there is a negative slant to Bolton's scheme. A bit of fatalism. Once begun, we're doomed to get more deeply involved — in any relationship — like it or not. And as we do, we lose our objectivity as well as our willingness to retreat if things go bad.

But, there are times when hanging in there may be best. Even if we feel stuck. In my church situation, I needed to be assured that I had given it my best shot before backing off. I'm so glad I did.

Similarly, our friends have a physically-handicapped son. They are committed to his well-being, in spite of enormous time and monetary costs. Stuck? Without a doubt. But, stuck in loving care and responsible servanthood!

Likewise, wives stick it out with husbands who seemingly have no interest in a healthy, growing relationship. For them, marriage is more than commitment, it is covenant.

Similarly, kids persist in classes where teachers are "impossible." They're building character. Parishioners wait it out, hoping that their minister will improve or move. The same is true of employees with "heartless" bosses, and home dwellers with impossible neighbors.

When the decision to bail out is based on convenience, persistence is the rule. As Christians, we're called upon to "go the extra mile in love." People can change — and often do. Prayer and patience are powerful.

But, the truth still remains: There are limits. Some relationships become hopelessly intolerable. Lives begin to disintegrate, e.g., spousal abuse. To just drift along, seeing dangerous deterioration, is to be unwise. Something must be done. But what?

It's Time to Chart Our Direction

Some time ago I saw some old World War II footage that featured the "Bataan Death March." Allied captives were being shoved with rifle butts. They had no choice, wounded or not, but to keep moving on.

Likewise, whenever we're being pushed, we're in a rather helpless position. We feel force from behind, and find ourselves lunging in a certain direction. Furthermore, it is very possible that our momentum will land us in some ditch or gully. Why? Because we're off balance. We're being made to go in a direction we don't wish to go.

The imagery applies to the inhospitable shove of unexpected and unwanted circumstances that are beyond our control. We can be thrown off balance, lose our psychological (and even spiritual) footing, and end up in a relationship predicament. Stuck ever so fast.

Before unwrapping possible solutions for our plight let's, in retrospect, pause to reflect on a few questions prompted by our discussion so far. Grab a pencil and provide thoughtful answers.

1. After reviewing which "animal" I most resemble, how has this temperament pushed me into getting stuck with people?

2. When have I chosen to be stuck for a good reason? Am I glad, now, that I hung in there? Why?

3. Have I ever remained stuck when I should have become free (e.g., abusive relationship)?

4. In addition to the "push circumstances" we have discussed, can I think of others in my life?

Choosing an Escape Route

"Any direction, just so it be forward!"
(General George Custer)
"The longest journey begins with one step."
(Ancient Chinese Proverb)
"When you come to a fork in the road, take it."
(Yogi Berra)

In the minds of many, Malibu is synonymous with perpetual paradise. Heaven on earth. Nirvana. Its picturesque beauty is considered unparalleled, with a mesmerizing "string of pearls" coastline at sunset.

Recent events make this idyllic image seem suspect. On the heels of 150 foot flames that incinerated scores of hillside homes, and just after the devastating 6.8 earthquake, down came the heavy rains — along with incredible mudslides. These unwelcome "guests" slid onto our Pepperdine campus like black serpents, covering cars, roads, and everything else in their pathway.

Though messy and inconvenient, mud was less threatening than the gigantic rocks that perch, perilously, on top of our coastal mountains.

Recently, a several-ton boulder plunged onto the

roof of a car ahead of mine, and crushed it like a tin can. The passenger, one of our students, was fortunate to have only sustained a broken collar bone. She offered gratitude to God on the 6 o'clock news, while being wheeled to surgery.

On more than one occasion, these treacherous conditions caused all roads to be barricaded. Result: Options for getting home were almost nil.

I could have taken a chance, broken the law, and tried to plow through the barriers. But, to do so would have been to risk arrest or, worse yet, the fate of the student.

Or, I could have remained at school, and "bunked" for the night. But, that would have meant wearing the same clothes the following day, and being separated from my beautiful wife.

Of course, I might have purchased a helicopter or boat, and circumvented all barriers. Great idea! All I'd have to do is mortgage our home!

Obviously, none of these options was realistic.

Fact: Roadblocks can make life pretty miserable. When we're locked in, immobilized, and cut off, we are incapacitated. We're super stuck!

Do we feel helpless? Does the pope own rosary beads? Both answers are identical. Do we become more than a tad frustrated? You bet. Especially when our roadblocks involve relationships with others. When frustrations soar and we simply can't get through. No matter how sincere or intelligent we are. No matter how hard we try, love or even pray.

Time to Pick Up and Dust Off

I once heard about a basketball player who performed very poorly in a key game. His livid coach called "time out," walked over to the young man, and yelled: "Don't just do something, stand there!"

For those of us who face unresolvable situations, eventually, we must advise ourselves to do the opposite. We must do something, as my coach used to say, "even if it's wrong." Remaining stationary won't cut it.

Somehow, we must find a way to cope effectively. After reacting to trauma, pain, frustration and healthy grieving, it's time to redirect attention toward a solution-goal. An "escape route" that can lead us to resolution and even restoration.

The alternative roads available are displayed on this chart. As each is briefly described, let's reflect on the ones we've tried, along with the results. And while doing this, let's allow ourselves to recall faces, places and memorable events from our life story.

POTENTIAL ESCAPE ROUTES

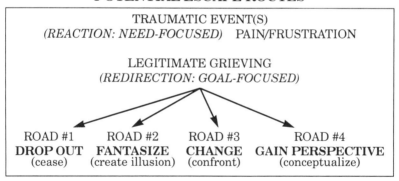

Road #1
"Tossing in the Towel"

When Dan Quayle bowed out of the 1996 Presidential derby, one cartoon pictured him in boyish attire, holding up a large block-lettered sign that read: ***I QUITE!***

Sometimes we choose to quit, give up, cash in, hang it up. In lawyer parlance we've decided to "cease and desist"; in boxer lingo, we've opted to "toss in the towel." In short, we've had it up to here, and see no apparent reason to continue trying.

But, there's a bit more to this option than we might think.

There are times when we can't walk away. Like the fly on the flypaper, our mobility is severely restricted. We're beached. We are compelled to continue facing the same tyrannical boss, unreasonable spouse, insistent bill collectors, inescapable health condition.

Each day feels like a week's worth. The pressures relentlessly pound, like storm-driven waves on a sea wall. But, again, we're not about to escape and we know it. Like it or not, we're stuck for the long haul.

Other times we really could, and should, quit but refuse to do so. Baseball managers, college administrators, politicians, and ministers often have tenures that exceed their effectiveness. Either they choose to ignore reality, to cease trying, or both.

To hang on until things really unravel is detrimental both for others and ourselves. Nevertheless, to relinquish — hands-down — can be extremely difficult. Ask any "empty nest" parents, who have just bid farewell to their college-bound daughter or son.

In other instances, we should drop out and we do. We're convinced that it is highly advisable to back out, to close shop, to confidently walk away with our head held high. We've received guidance from our heavenly Father, trusted friends, or our conscience — and boldly chosen to "cut bait" with a completely irresolvable, or draining situation. We've asked ourselves: "Who needs more of this?" and responded by taking courageous backward steps. As a result, we have closure and can get on with life.

But it seems like, most frequent of all, are the times we shouldn't quit but do. We flake out, betraying commitments and letting the chips fall.[1] Indeed, far too many drop out too fast. The second we feel our "comfort zone" is being trespassed. When we think that demands and responsibilities have become a bit much. When we feel squeezed-in, inconvenienced, overloaded.

Our world is filled with people who shirk their responsibilities. Like "deadbeat dads" — divorced fathers who abrogate their court-decreed responsibility to support their offspring. Or moms, who suddenly trash families to "find themselves." (I counseled one who, with a cavalier attitude, torpedoed the psychological well-being of her four children.)

Then there are those who, for their own reasons,

---

1. A recent article in the *L.A. Times*, entitled "The Flake Factor," explains that our society is inundated with an ever-increasing number of flakes — persons who do not keep commitments. They always make excuses, sometimes apologize, but never improve.

A key reason for flakiness: a culture that favors "factoids" (easy-to-access, "mind-numbing junk food of information") over facts. Included under the factoid umbrella are mind-dazing activities like: vegging on TV, absorbing nonsensical lyrics, counting advertisements in magazines and delving into forums on the Internet.

Other reasons for being flaky? People are too tired, busy and worried about money. They get psychic overload and, as a result, seek diversions to avoid focusing on serious commitments.

According to researchers Bruce Feld and Cris Evatt, a survey of 1,000 couples revealed that men are nine times more likely to be flakes than women. (*L.A. Times*, 3/27/95, pp. E-3, E-5, by Kristina Sauerwein).

"hit the skids" in their Christian faith. No longer do they accept the Bible as their guide. No longer do they care to be around spiritual people. All things become new, but in the wrong sense.

He was my soulmate when we were both teenagers. We did everything together. Had a ton of fun but also shared meaningful worship experiences. In biblical terms, we were "of like mind." More like brothers than brothers. Then we parted: He to med school — then the navy; me to grad school.

Several years later we got together. Right off the bat I noticed the change. He seemed eager to share his "new insights." During his military stint in Guam, he was introduced to eastern religions. No longer was Christ unique nor Christianity special. A large Buddha now stood in the entry way of his home!

Essentially, my buddy was no longer a believer. The greatest thing that had bonded us suddenly disappeared. He had dropped out, and our relationship seemed doomed.

How could this have possibly occurred? Why had he considered his Christian faith no more permanent than a jacket — something casually shed at will?

Then the light went on. My friend, now a successful doctor, had chosen glitz — the trappings of affluence. Jettisoning his childhood faith, considered too generic and incompatible with his high status, he embraced a new, avant-garde "designer" faith. One that made him seem a cut above the masses.

My old sidekick succumbed to empty, false enticements. He axed his religious roots, and dropped out on Jesus. Result: Our relationship was, indeed, never quite the same — that is, until he later contracted incurable cancer.

As I shared prayers and Scriptures at his bedside, the spark of truth rekindled his heart. Then, at his funeral, his cousin affirmed that he was heaven (not Nirvana!) bound!

We choose to drop out for a host of reasons: doubt, discouragement, fatigue. But, these are usually derived from feeling thoroughly bogged down.

Question: Is quitting a recommended option? Allow me to propose this rule-of-thumb: Unless thought through very carefully, and prayerfully, it's usually not preferable. Why?

A. Things can turn around. (As Oswald Chambers declared, God can change the most unfavorable circumstances in an eyeblink!)

B. Jesus can show us a creative solution, one we could never predict. (After Paul journeyed to Troas he declares: *"the Lord . . .opened a door for me."* 2 Cor. 2:12. He can do that for all of us.)

C. There is great merit — when possible — in hanging tough in hope. (Heb. 12:1 says: *". . .let us run with perseverance the race marked out for us."* Then, in verse 11: *"No discipline seems pleasant at the time, but painful. Later on, however, it produces a harvest of righteousness and peace for those who have been trained by it."*)

It's usually better to face the music. To accept and responsibly deal with reality. To not succumb to the pervasive, attractive temptation to quit.

In a word, rather than "throwing in the towel," it's usually better to simply grip it a little tighter!

Road #2
Wishing upon a Star

The well-known Disney refrain goes:

"When we wish upon a star, makes no difference
who we are."

Our fantasizing rarely involves simply wishing,
rather, it more frequently involves:
1. blocking (or dulling) our pain with artificial
   stimulants (e.g., pills, alcohol, food); or,
2. telling ourselves "lies" (e.g., making excuses,
   twisting the interpretation of past events).

In both cases, we resort to pretending that things
aren't as bad as we know them to be. Psychologists
term this "denial," and assure us that it is most
intense when circumstances are considered the most
devastating.

It is little wonder that our most-loved fairy tales
were written in times and places of destitution, political threat, and uncertainty. There existed a felt desperate need to "play make-believe" — especially
when explaining life to innocent children. And the
residual thought was always, as in Disney's song:
Who knows, "our wish just may come true."

Today, trouble rages in our land. Many of us feel
frightened, angry or alone. To make our lives seem
more kind and gentle, we grab onto certain "fantasy
myths" floating around. Chuck Swindoll mentions
four:
1. *"Laugh and the world laughs with you. Cry and
   you cry alone."* (The opposite seems more accurate!)
2. *"There's a light at the end of every tunnel. Keep
   hoping . . . keep looking for it."* (More likely, it's
   the headlamp of an oncoming freight train!)
3. *"Every day in every way our world is getting better."* (Give me a break. Most everyone bought
   into this myth just before World War II began.)

4. *"Things never are as bad as they seem."* (They're incredibly worse!)[2]

When locked into one of life's "catch 22s," it is extremely tempting to fantasize. To pretend. To make-up idealized scenarios, and cling to them for dear life — at least until we're better able to cope with resulting stress and pain.

Furthermore, at times, some fantasy seems justified — especially, the "wouldn't-it-be-nice-if" kind. Maxwell Maltz, in his bestseller of a previous era, *Psycho-Cybernetics*, highly recommends dreaming. According to him, dreams become raw materials for constructing better realities. Usually they are the precedents to improvements.[3]

If nothing else, fantasizing helps cure boredom. Life can become dull. H.L. Mencken says, "The basic fact about human experience is not that it is a tragedy, but that it is a bore." Thoreau bluntly declares, "Most (people) lead lives of quiet desperation."[4] Boredom can extinguish our life energy and enjoyment. A touch of "Disneyland," now and then, can perk us up. Get our juices flowing again.

A key problem occurs when fantasy becomes a means of permanent avoidance. A way of escaping painful impasses, by pretending they do not exist. This only sets us up for further disappointment and trauma.

For example, when we convince ourselves that all

---

2. Charles R. Swindoll, *Living on the Ragged Edge: Coming to Terms with Reality* (Waco, TX: Word Books, 1985), p. 24.

3. Maxwell Maltz, *Psycho-Cybernetics: A New Way to Get More Living Out of Life* (Hollywood, CA: Wilshire Book Company, 1960).

4. Swindoll, p. 25.

sickness will get better, all people are well-intentioned, all nations really want peace. With such elevated expectations, we're bound to experience an eventual, not-so-gentle, letdown — otherwise known as a "crash!"

Some new Christians I've known, are devastated when they discover rampant nepotism, cronyism and elitism within the church. They say: "The church simply isn't like this. I must be reading it the wrong way." As their fantasy-bubble deflates, they're forced to face realities that run counter to their expectations and wishes. In short, they "hit the wall" — and are forced to deal with the facts.

A second difficulty looms when our hopes, or hurts, cause us to blur the distinction between truth and fiction. Let me illustrate.

My wife's friend recently divorced. Her life has become fantasy run amok!

➤ She imagines her former husband to be homosexual — though they have a child and he has remarried.

➤ Wishfully, she contends that his new marriage is heading toward the rocks. To hear her, it'll "tank" soon.

➤ She idealizes all males who show her the slightest bit of attention. In her mind they're Greek gods, who are dying to date her.

Fantasy, for her, is a drug. In fact it's a couple of them — an anesthetic to dull pain, and a brisk stimulant to generate hope.

Bottom line: Is fantasy good for us? At times, you bet. Other times, well, it can be severely counterproductive. Whenever we possibly can, our Lord wants us to recognize and face up to reality. Only then can we begin to firmly grab onto the "handle of cope," in addition to the one of "hope."

Road #3
Where There's a Will . . . .

From sea-to-shining-sea, this nation abounds with fair-haired, grinning, motivational speakers. Their messages converge on a few central themes, illustrated in these statements:

> "Failure is never final. We must never think of ourselves as a 'failure' but, rather, as a 'novice-in-training.'"

> "The only difference between the difficult and impossible is: the impossible takes a little longer for us to accomplish."

> "Like the turtle, we only make progress when we stick our neck out."

The key idea comes through loud and clear: No bad situation need ever be permanent; by our efforts we can always change things for the better. Not by fantasizing, but by sheer effort — guided by wisdom.

This "bootstraps" notion often assumes that, when changes for the better do not occur, it's our fault. Either we lack the correct formula or the necessary commitment. Our only option is, like the proverbial bull in the arena, to take a few paces backward and charge again, again, and again.

Enough hard, snorting charges and eventually things are bound to improve.

But in reality, our hearts tell us that some conditions are extremely resistant to improvement. Put simply, they are chronically bad.

In a faculty conference, I once heard Oregon's

Senator, Mark Hatfield, respond to this question: "Can dedicated Christian leaders reform Washington D.C.'s moral climate?" His answer: "Not really. The forces of evil are just too firmly entrenched." Several chafed at his response.

In this book, our main concern is irreconcilable differences, unresolvable difficulties, incredible dilemmas. Situations that many of us have, indeed, tried to squirm out of.

We've tried everything in the book to bring about change. Nothing seems to work. We're locked in tightly. Suffocated. Strangled. Totally exasperated. Now what?

Admittedly, even the most unexpected change is possible. History is filled with *"Who Would Have Ever Believed . . ."* instances — recently, the Berlin Wall's dismemberment, PLO-Israeli peace accord, IRA-British reconciliation talks, etc.

Furthermore, change can remain our eventual goal.

Nevertheless, to continue hoping and struggling for improvement to occur is, often, not in our best interest. Rather, we should accept the immutability of some things — and not be demolished by that admission. We can still survive, learn, hope. (It's even okay to believe that the "final chapter" may not yet be written in stone.)

The "Serenity Prayer" of Alcoholics Anonymous says it all: "God grant me serenity to accept the things I cannot change, courage to change the things I can, and wisdom to know the difference."[5]

---

5. "A Serenity Prayer," from a sermon by Reinhold Niebuhr (1934), entitled "For A Congregational Church." The original version is as follows:

Good advice? Ask Mary, who sat in my office to receive counseling. She was seriously considering suicide, because she couldn't get her husband to change his ways. She had tried the two steps that most of us take, when seeking to improve (or save) a relationship:

1. attempt to **change** the other person;
2. try to **communicate** with the other person — even though immediate change seems unlikely.

She admitted to having failed on both counts. But, that was only "strike two." Having one more strike to go, she "took a serious swing" at learning how to **cope**. And was she ever glad she did!

By directing her attention to *coping* skills, rather than on improvements that appeared unlikely, she began making real progress. Mary is still living, and happens to be functioning well. Furthermore, to her amazement and gratitude, that "impossible" husband is making headway — though, admittedly, his rate of change is a real study in incrementology!

Undeniably, at times striving for change is a preferable road.

Other times, it's a detour to futility. In such

"God grant me serenity to accept the things I cannot change,
Courage to change the things I can, and
Wisdom to know the difference.
Living one day at a time,
enjoying one moment at a time;
Accepting hardship as a pathway to peace;
Taking, as Jesus did, this sinful world as it is,
not as I would have it;
Trusting that You will make all things right if I surrender
to Your will;
So that I may be reasonably happy in this life and
supremely with You forever in the next."

instances, we're far better to focus on coping, on getting on with life, rather than remaining stuck — depending on another person's (or a situation's) improvement.

Consulting Our Map for a "Road Less Traveled"

We've driven down three roads, and discovered that they lead us nowhere — more lost, stranded and stuck than ever. Why?

> ➤ dropping out seems too much like copping out;
> ➤ fantasizing appears to push us too far away from reality;
> ➤ intensifying effort produces zilch — due to set conditions or resistant human wills.

Now it's time to focus on the road that's certain to get us unstuck. A sleek, smooth "interstate highway" that truly allows us to escape oppressive persons and unsolvable situations. So that we're equipped to cope in a clearminded and warmhearted way.

Here's a hint: This road has everything to do with what, and how well, we see.

But, before proceeding, pause in retrospect, and jot down your responses to these questions:

1. **When, in my past life, did I "throw in the towel?" (When was this premature and unwise? When was it, probably, the best course of action?)**

2. **When have I resorted to fantasy and denial? (Why did this kind of response surface? Was it justified, given the situation you faced? Did it subside?)**

3. Have I ever attempted to improve someone, or a situation, by sheer dogged persistence or by manipulation? (What valuable lessons did I learn? Based on this experience, under what conditions should a person give up trying?)

4. In addition to the three roads mentioned so far, which others have I (or persons near me) tried? (What have the anticipated results been? The unanticipated results?)

Take a Good Look!

"The heart has eyes which the brain knows nothing of."
(Hans Margolius)
"Vision clears as the silt drops from the current of our life."
(Charles R. Swindoll)
"Lord, if you can't make me look thin,
make my friends look fat."
(Erma Bombeck)

Hats off to bats! Humans owe them a huge apology. Sure, they're not the beauty queens of God's creation. Pictures of them frighten children on Halloween: with their furry bodies, skin-covered wings, and strange habit of hanging upside down in spooky caves.

Most of us would prefer caressing a kitten, or stroking the nose of a thoroughbred, than coming within 100 yards of a bat. That goes for all 900 species of these black critters!

Nevertheless, bats have received unfair press. They are repeatedly described as sightless.[1] The

---

1. The eyes of bats are, indeed, useless at night. Nocturnal navigation occurs by "echolocation," which is based on the sonar principle. Tragi (small lobes near each ear opening) and nose leaves (membranous appendages hanging from nostrils and ears)

phrase, "blind as a bat," is as universally accepted as statements depicting foxes sly and owls wise. But, in reality, bats see as well as we — although most have tiny eyes concealed by fur.

Why does this misconception doggedly persist? Maybe it's because we tend to believe demeaning untruths about anything ugly. More likely, we're "bat incompetents" because we rarely see any. We prefer shopping malls and sports stadiums — places where bats don't (excuse the expression) "hang out."

Sight: Our Golden Gateway to Reality

It all comes down to what our "clappers" behold. To see is, indeed, to know. Sight is our gateway to understanding, but also to competence, enjoyment, awareness. Its value cannot be overstated.

With eyes, we maximize potential for living full, rich, quality lives. God's universe impacts us with its incredible beauty, and we are enabled to employ its rich resources for great personal benefit.[2]

---

emit supersonic sounds. These are reflected as echoes off nearby objects, and are picked up by their sensory apparatus. Results: bats ascertain positions of walls, trees, etc. in order to avoid collisions. (George H.H. Tate, *Encyclopedia Americana International Edition*, Vol. 2. Danbury, CT: Grolier Inc., 1984, p. 340.)

2. "*Vision* is a highly complex process, in which light rays entering the eye are focused on the retina where they are converted into nerve impulses that are then coded and carried to the brain (through the optic nerve).

"Each ganglion cell produces a nerve fiber that travels from the cell body to the optic disk, an area located in the nasal half of the eye. In this area, known as the 'blind spot,' the nerve fibers leading to the brain have displaced all other retina cells so that this region is insensitive to light. From the optic disk, the nerve fibers, forming a single large nerve known as the 'optic nerve,' pass through the choroid sclera, and bony socket to

> Ask *Ted Williams* — baseball's immortal slugger — the last player to top .400 in batting average.[3] His eyes could follow a 98 m.p.h. fastball to the point of bat contact!

> Ask *lunar astronauts*, whose spaceship orbits on the back side of the moon — so they lose sight of earth. What relief they must feel when visual contact is regained!

> Ask *Ray Charles*, forced to overcome the limitations of sightlessness — or Pepperdine psychology students, who learn to better appreciate sight by agreeing to wear a blindfold (and be led around) for one full day.

Again, our ability to see well exponentially expands the quality of our lives. It's the road that will get us unstuck, as well as take us to rewarding destinations. Let me explain.

The "P" Word

To begin, it is important to understand that sight and perspective are two "chunks" of the same reality. Both refer to the means whereby we feed our minds with visual images and messages.

The distinction? In a word, perspective focuses on the quality and depth of our sight. It's very close to

---

enter the brain. Each optic nerve contains about one million nerve fibers." (*Enclyclopedia Americana, Deluxe Library Edition*, Vol. 10, Danbury, CT: Grolier, Incorporated, 1991, p. 812).

3. Ted Williams batted .406 during the 1941 season. Later, during the Korean War, his exceptional sight enabled him to fly many successful bombing missions. Upon his return, much to the regret of opposing pitchers, he resumed his incredible performance at the plate.

what we understand as insight. Sometimes it appears as foresight. Or even hindsight.

Charles Swindoll declares:

> *"Most of us have better sight than insight. There's nothing wrong with our vision, it's perspective that throws us a curve. We see the obvious, but overlook the significant. We focus on the surface, but fail to see what is deep."*[4]

To illustrate, we might see only a block of marble, but Michelangelo would envision the same rock with perspective. He once declared: "Carving an angel out of stone is not difficult for me. After 'seeing' the angel, I simply cut away that part that is not the angel." Now that's perspective!

Again, Swindoll provides this illuminating description of the concept:

*"The term literally suggests **"looking through . . . seeing clearly."** One who views life through perspective lenses has the capacity to see things in their relative importance."*[5]

Such a person, according to this author, has an accurate assessment of the big picture. A picture that he sees contextually (how it blends into its setting) and creatively (ways it can be interpreted).

The artist devoid of perspective is, in Shakespeare's words, *"weary, stale, flat, and unprofitable."* The leader without it is intimidated, vulnerable, and potentially a slave to public opinion and to his fears. The athlete minus it cannot get beyond his playbook.

---

4. Charles R. Swindoll, *Living on the Ragged Edge: Coming to Terms with Reality*, (Waco, TX: Word Books, 1985), p. 53.

5. Charles R. Swindoll, *Come Before Winter, And Share My Hope* (Portland: Multnomah Press, 1988), p. 327.

Would you believe it? Perspective can even boost the morale of a kid. I recently heard about a five-year-old, who kept striking at the baseball he tossed up. His older brother disparagingly yelled: "You're sure a lousy hitter!" Without batting an eye, the small-fry shot back: "Nope. I'm just a fantastic pitcher!"

Gaining perspective promises to add a breath of fresh air to the all suffocating demands of our lives. Guaranteed! It opens new dimensions, and enables us to cope effectively. It eases the tyranny of the urgent. It provides psychological shock absorbers.

When perspective arrives on the scene something phenomenal occurs.

Life becomes a symphony. A captivating poem. A personal affirmation. Put another way:

> *"The chips of insignificance fall away as the broad images of truth emerge in the monuments of our minds. We begin to see more clearly as the fog lifts. . .and we are running no (faster) . (N)or confused. (N)or angry. (N)or overwhelmed."*[6]

Perspective. We all need a ton of it ASAP! Especially when we find ourselves submerged in relationship impasses. Stuck with uncaring, unimproving, even unapproachable persons. Locked into misery. Unable to budge, and for no fault of our own.

After we've given it our best shot, and it backfired! After we've dropped out. Or conned ourselves into believing things weren't so bad. Or ratcheted up our courage to try harder. Nevertheless, we remain stuck.

Perspective promises to help us rise above our

---

6. Ibid.

frustration. To envision a future with hope.[7] To be at peace.

And, here's something else, to enable us to place ourselves in the very best strategic position for the eventual improvement of our circumstances. To maximize the results if (or when) things turn around.

The old sage was right on target when he declared: *"Life is 10 percent what happens to us and 90 percent how we envision it."* How it computes with us. What spin we give it.

How do I write with such assurance? Personal experience. Renewed perspective worked wonders in my life. After trudging along bogus roads, I asked God to help me see my traumatic church experience from a more positive and constructive vantage point. And He did.

It made all the difference in the world.

Suddenly, down deep inside, I just knew that things would be okay — in spite of painful memories, fears, insecurities, doubts.

Put another way: The angel inside of that rough

---

7. Webster defines *"hope"*: "to desire with expectation of fulfillment." To hope is to anticipate. More than dreaming, it's possessing within ourselves an expectation of fulfilled desires. Hope is "always on tiptoes," looking to the future. It makes a dismal today bearable because of its promise for a brighter tomorrow. Without it, something inside dies.

The Greek term for "hope" connotes a similar meaning: *"favorable and confident expectation."* The *Good News Bible* renders Prov. 13:12: *"When hope is crushed, the heart is crushed, But a wish come true fills you with joy."* The *New American Standard Bible* says: *"Hope deferred makes the heart sick, but desire fulfilled is a tree of life."* The Hebrew term *Chalah* (translated *"sick"*) implies a heart being crushed. Charles A. Swindoll, *Dropping Your Guard: The Value Of Open Relationships* (Waco, TX: Word Books, 1983), pp. 192-193.

and grotesque substance became visible. Furthermore, my heavenly Father chiseled away all the clutter until the angel was free.

It is obvious that I didn't simply choose just another perspective. One that seemed novel and promising. The world offers a telephone book full of perspectives, each tailor-made for any desire. New pop psychology books, offering instant results, continuously appear — and their authors speak authoritatively on TV talk shows. But, none of these enticed me.

My new perspective was anchored in a firm belief of God's ability, and willingness, to help me improve my sight. To provide me with new optical capacity.

And with my "new eyes," I was confident that I'd draw new, helpful conclusions. About my significance, my existence, my surroundings. Expected results? I'd get unstuck.

And He didn't let me down. In fact, He went overboard in His generosity — which is not unlike Him. You see, His gift of insight spilled over into the other areas of my life, so that now I'm much better able to comprehend how everything fits together. What a quintessential blessing!

Question: Speaking of God, what about His sight and perspective? How do (or should) they interface with ours? Did Jesus offer specific teaching regarding our eyes?

In seeking answers, let's "surf" into some spiritual truth.

Our Divine Monitor

First, we can comfort ourselves by realizing that seeing is God's specialty. He continuously

looks at us. Not because He is snoopy, trying to catch us failing. Nor because He is bored, and doesn't have better things to occupy His time and attention. There's only one reason: He truly cares. He has our interests at heart.

The Old Testament reveals that our compassionate Father watches us intently — just as our earthly fathers pin their eyes on their lovable, though sometimes wandering, offspring. The writer of Proverbs puts it succinctly: *"The eyes of the Lord are everywhere, keeping watch on the wicked and the good"* (15:3).[8]

What else does He look at? His Word explains.

He *sees* injustice (Lam. 3:34), the death of His prophet (2 Chron. 24:22), the distress of His own (Exod. 3:7). He *looks for* faithfulness (Ps. 101:6), and for trust (Jer 5:3). He, also, has His *Eyes on* the sinful kingdom (Amos 9:8). Man cannot hide (Ps. 139:3,7, 16). God *sees* into his innermost being (1 Sam. 16:7).[9]

What is the point? God's perspective is all-inclusive and intense. But once again, above all, it is supremely compassionate, unlike the ancient Mayan gods that I observed in the "holy chambers" atop Guatemala's pyramids. Their dispassionate, stone eyes gaze away into the distance — totally unconcerned for the human sacrifices made by lowly worshipers.[10]

---

8. *Dictionary Of New Testament Theology*, Colin Brown, ed., vol 3, "Pri-Z," Grand Rapids: Zondervan Publishers, 1986, pp. 513-514.

9. Ibid.

10. When the Mayan Empire dominated Central America, human sacrifice was rampant. With students, my wife and I journeyed to Yucatan, Mexico, and parts of Guatemala, to

In sharp contrast, our God looks intently. He sees everything — the big picture. And with that capacity, who could possibly be more qualified to help us correct, sharpen and correct our vision?

Spiritual Sight: A Gift from God

Second, in a spiritual sense, we must see God. His nature. His purposes. His track record. His love. Our eyes must, somehow, take in the full measure of His Being.

The Psalmist invites us to look at Him. We read: "*taste and see that the Lord is good* (34:8)."

"Day By Day," the favorite song from the musical *Godspell* entreats us to:

➤ **see** God more clearly;
➤ **follow** God more nearly;
➤ **love** God more dearly — day by day.

Note the sequence. Following and loving are preceded by envisioning.

But how can we see Him more clearly? Only one way: By asking Him to gift us with this special ability. Clara H. Scott's ageless hymn makes such a request:

> Open mine eyes, that I might see
> Glimpses of truth Thou hast for me;

---

observe the ruins of their once-flourishing cities.

Dominating such sites are pyramids, upon which were "god chambers," housing one or more stone deity(ies). Each had a flat, carved-out niche on his stomach. Worshipers would rip out human hearts from bodies of war captives and, while still palpitating, place them (as an offering) on the "plate" of the gods. They believed that, without this practice, the sun would freeze in the heavens, seasons would cease, and all would perish.

However, they believed that their gods remained unimpressed. That is why they are depicted as disinterestedly looking into the distance.

Place in my hands the wonderful key
That shall unclasp, and set me free.

Silently now I wait for Thee,
Ready, my God, Thy will to see.
Open my eyes, illumine me,
Spirit divine![11]

This is not a futile request. The Ruler of our universe, indeed, allows Himself to be seen, disclosed, revealed. He warmly invites us to scrutinize Him closely. Why? Because He knows that our gazing at Him is certain to result in our following Him more nearly — and loving Him more dearly — day-by-day.

Christ's Plan for Preventative Eye Maintenance

Third, Jesus teaches us extremely valuable lessons concerning the eye. It was a central theme for Him, as well as for the surrounding Greek culture.[12]

---

11. "Open My Eyes" by Clara H. Scott, *Sing to the Lord Hymnal*, Kansas City, MO: Lillenas Publishing, (song published 1895), 1993, p. 461.

12. The verbs of *"seeing"* and *"beholding,"* in Greek, have religious and philosophical significance. They considered the eye to be the source of knowledge. The scientific approach — emphasizing the acquisition of truth through the senses — first germinated in this society.

Greek religion was a religion of seeing. In contrast to Judaism, the role of hearing is subordinate to that of seeing. The Greeks were, truly, *"a people of the eye."*

The Greeks exerted a profound influence on New Testament writers. This explains why there are so many words associated with seeing. Sight imagery is plentiful and rich in significance — as it relates to our Christian walk.

The key word, *horao*, means *"see"* or *"perceive."* In its various

Furthermore, it is evident that, for Him, "eye correction" meant "perspective improvement." Pure and simple.

In His Sermon on the Mount, Jesus referred to the eye as the "lamp of the body." His point: The way we see determines whether our inner spirits are illuminated. His explanation (Matt. 6:22-23) is refreshingly clear in this paraphrase by Eugene H. Peterson:

> *Your eyes are windows into your body. If you open your eyes wide in wonder and belief, your body fills up with light. If you live squinty-eyed in greed and distrust, your body is a dark cellar. If you pull the blinds on your windows, what a dark light you will have.*[13]

Today (as in His day) so many are blinded; multitudes possess astigmatism. Result: There is a superabundance of fuzzy thinking and frustrated, misguided

---

forms, it is used no fewer than 110 times! Often the term is employed in a literal sense.

➤ Paul says to the Romans, "*I long to **see** you*" (11:1, emphasis added).

➤ Peter declares a prophecy: "*Whoever would love life and **see** good days must keep his tongue from evil and his lips from deceitful speech*" (1 Pet. 3:10).

➤ In John 16:16 Jesus declares to His disciples: "*In a little while you will **see** me no more, and then after a little while you will **see** me.*"

Sometimes, this Greek term is used figuratively. In explaining why He chose to speak to the people in parables, Jesus said: "*Though **seeing**, they do not **see***" (Matt. 13:13a). Obviously, "*see*" in the second use implies understanding, grasping or realizing. In short, they see with eyes — but not with their hearts. Somehow, it just doesn't click. *Dictionary Of New Testament Theology*, op. cit., pp. 513-514.

13. Eugene H. Peterson, *The Message: New Testament And Psalms* (Colorado Springs: Navpress, 1994).

living. People "see" it one way — the wrong way. Theirs is a world of illusion. Of distortion. Of blurry sight. And this sends them down the wrong road — one that's certain to get them stuck.

We are admonished, in no uncertain biblical terms, to see. And, what's more, to see *clearly* — 20/20 spiritual vision. If we truly see accurately — we'll be able to separate the incidental from the essential . . . the temporary from the eternal . . . the partial from the whole . . . the trees from the forest.[14]

The question hits us squarely: What is the condition of our eyes — the "lamps" that lighten our inner spirits? Are we in need of transplants, because we're blind? Or, will corrective lenses suffice, to clear up our distortion?

The point is clear: Few needs rival the one for clear sight — sight which offers side benefits of insight and foresight. We desperately need accurate, realistic perspective — perspective that leads to awareness and sensitivity.

By now it's clear; my appeal is for us to possess authentic "Christian perspective." That special brand exemplified by Jesus Christ. The exact kind that He desires for us who proudly carry His banner.

While on this earth, our Savior advocated some very radical sight remedies. Recall His "log removal" prescription?

> *"You hypocrite, first take the plank out of your own eye, and then you will see clearly to remove the speck from your brother's eye"* (Matt. 7:5).

On another occasion, his advice was more moderate. He admonished His disciples: *"Open your eyes*

---

14. Charles R. Swindoll, *Come Before Winter*.

and look at the fields! They are ripe for harvest" (John 4:35).

For some of us, gigantic logs block our vision. For others, we need only open our eyes wider and look at more. In either case, our eyesight can drastically improve.

In essence, we are to look at life and the world *clearly*. That's a commendable first step. But, in addition, we must increasingly see *rightly*. We must envision our surroundings from His vantage point.

But how, specifically, is it acquired? Do only the lucky attain such an extraordinary perspective by accident? Does it emerge when we work, or become clever, enough? Or, perhaps, when we discipline ourselves to the max?

In short, how do we get from where many of us are — stuck in the mire of shortsightedness and unresolvable dilemmas — to the rich, green-clovered plateau of perspective?

It is to that crucial concern that we now direct our attention.

Pausing to Reflect

But, before bidding this chapter adieu, let's take time to respond to these penetrating questions. It will do us good.

1. **Have I had occasion to have special appreciation for my ability to see? When? If not, why do I seem to take this gift for granted?**

2. Do I have perspective (depth of insight/foresight) in (a) certain area(s)? What area(s)? What produced it? How has it been useful? How do others respond?

3. How has a renewed, or changed, perspective helped me to overcome an impasse with another person? To rise above it? To overcome?

4. To what extent have I ever "seen" God? What did I see? Have I ever sensed that God was looking at me? When?

Gaining Sight

CHAPTER FIVE

A Quick Rest Stop

*"It is not imperative that we see eye-to-eye, but it is
absolutely necessary that we walk arm-in-arm."*
(Earl Lee)
"Vision is the art of seeing the invisible."
(Louis T. Mann)
"In the country of the blind, the one-eyed man is king."
(Erasmus)

We've wisely chosen to travel on the "Christian
Perspective Highway." We're cruising past ditches,
roadblocks and all kinds of hazards. If we can just
keep going, we'll be home free.

But, travel can make us weary. Periodic rest stops
are a must. Just as they were when our family took
long vacations during my childhood.

My father preferred to start at daybreak, and go
until late evening. Why? I'm not sure. Perhaps, it
meant fewer nights to pay for motels. Or he was pretending to be Mario Andretti!

The only entertainment on these excursions was
playing "alphabet signs," counting highway roadkill,
or fighting with my brother.

How we'd all look forward to those rest stops. The
times when we would spot a roadside park. One with

a few grassy spots, scattered trees and picnic tables.

Out would come the plastic table cloth, picnic basket and Coleman gas stove. Before long, we could smell the Spam cooking — as it splattered grease in all directions. The meals, spartan as they were, tasted great.

But, most of all, it was refreshing to take a break from being cramped up in a fetal position and feeling road vibrations. We would breathe deeply, and feel the cool grass between our toes.

Of course, there were the conversations. We would reflect on what we had seen that day. Then, on our "pit stop," we'd anticipate the sites just ahead.

In this book, we've covered some ground. In our mind's eye, let's jam on the brakes at this rest stop. Let's get out. Take a deep breath. Pump up the Coleman. Set the table. Eat heartily. And, then, let's summarize where we've been, and where we're heading.

A Glance Backward

We began by describing that "get stuck feeling." In particular, how the "misery index" soars when we're involved in relationship impasses. Times when we're convinced we're not at fault. When people, for whatever reason, just decide to get nasty. We feel helpless. Life seems hopeless — like a unsolved riddle. One big Rubik cube!

Then, we contemplated various ways we drift into such situations. So that we're victimized. Checkmated.

At this point, we focused on some possible escape routes. Four to be exact. We noted that the first three were less than ideal, though sometimes necessary — at least for awhile. But, the fourth, cultivating a new perspective, was seen as (by far) our best course.

The merits of renewed perspective were reviewed. More specifically, a truly Christian perspective was strongly advocated. Finally, we discussed how God and Jesus place priority on seeing clearly and rightly. Also, they provide us with nurturing guidance.

A Glimpse Forward

Having placed this theme before us, the question becomes: Where do we proceed from here? In particular, in what ways does God help us to attain renewed perspective — so that we can get (and stay) unstuck — so that those around us will recognize that our "eyes" are becoming like those of our compassionate heavenly Father? Gary Chapman's inspiring song, "Father's Eyes," describes what His are like:

> "Eyes that (find) the good in things
>   when good (is) not around.
> Eyes that (find) the Source of help
>   when help (cannot) be found.
> Eyes of compassion, seeing every pain
>   knowing what (people)
>   are going through and feeling it the same.
> Just like my Father's eyes."[1]

It is to that request we now turn our attention.

There are three ways that He helps us to gain perspective. To have His eyes. These are:

✧ PERSONAL REVELATION ✧

✧ PERCEPTION ✧

✧ POINT OF VIEW ✧

1. "Father's Eyes," from album by the same name, by Gary Chapman (Word Music, 1979).

Let's examine each closely in the next chapters.

It's time to throw all gear into the car and move on down the road.

CHAPTER SIX

Personal Revelation:
How V.S.P. Receive Sight

*"I would give all the wealth in the world,
and all the deeds of all heroes, for one true vision."*
(Henry David Thoreau)

*"Once I saw the truth there was nothing
I could do to unsee It."*
(Ancient Greek philosopher)

*"Two Foundation Facts Of Human Enlightenment:
1) There is a God. 2) You are NOT Him."*
(Source unknown)

Perhaps it is because he is my namesake. More likely, it's based on my visit to the remote and rocky Greek island of Patmos — upon which he was banished.

This 10 x 6 mile island, one of the smallest of the Aegean Sea, is located 60 miles southwest of Ephesus — off the coast of Asia Minor. Furthermore, it served as the Roman Empire's "Alcatraz Island." Pliny the Elder mentions it as a place of banishment, where exiles ("enemies of the Empire") remained until death.

The banishment that John experienced was, in all likelihood, accompanied by fetters, scanty clothing, insufficient food, sleeping on bare ground in a dark prison, and work under the lash of military over-seers.

Why was he there? At the time, emperor worship was the dominant religion. Furthermore, its rituals were not optional. All citizens must take an oath attesting to the "divine spirit" of the emperor, and offer incense and wine in honor of his "godhead." This was performed on the altar before his image.[1]

Christians were suspected of disloyalty. The fact that they often met secretly at night or at daybreak only served to make them seem more suspicious.

Typically, they were seized and dragged before the magistrates. Any who persisted in saying they were Christians (repeating it three times), were executed or banished. Those who recanted, by cursing Christ and worshiping the statues of the emperor-god, were released with a stern warning.

In this political climate, John was exiled to Patmos. His exile carried with it loss of civil rights and all loss of property.

Who was John? He refers to himself as Christ's servant, (Rev. 1:1) and calls himself a *"companion in . . . suffering"* with those to whom he is writing (Rev. 1:9). He was, in all probability, a Christian confessor who testified to his faith before Roman authorities.

As a prisoner on Patmos, he suffered tribulation — and with "patient endurance" waited for God's guidance.

Then it all happened in a flash. The incredible, prophetic vision occurred — as recorded in the Book of Revelation. Otto F.A. Meinardus terms it "probably

---

1. Otto F.A. Meinardus, *St. John of Patmos and the Seven Churches of the Apocalypse* (Athens: Lycabettus Press, 1974), pp. 1-2.

the least seriously studied and the most misunder-stood of all New Testament writings."[2]

Date with an Angel

The cave where it is believed to have occurred is on the side of a mountain. Called "The Grotto of the Apocalypse," this stone-faced enclosure is filled with holy vestments from past centuries. The large Monastery of Saint John towers above it.

A hushed quietness enveloped me as I stooped to enter. I tried to picture "the disciple Jesus loved," meditating on the Lord's Day — nearly 2,000 years ago. Let's hear him describe what occurred:

> *"I was in the Spirit, and I heard behind me a loud voice like a trumpet, which said: 'Write on a scroll what you see. . .'"* (Rev. 1:10-11).

Then, the images began to dramatically appear.

> *"When I turned I saw seven golden lampstands, and among the lampstands was someone like a son of man, dressed in a robe reaching down to*

---

2. "Today, people are intently focusing on issues related to survival. Does this ecstatic Seer, writing from the island of Patmos, have anything to say on this subject?

"Unfortunately, cranks have exploited the Revelation of John, to fit predetermined religious, political, and social desires. In so doing, they have greatly distorted its eternal truth.

"A word about Patmos. Much is known about John, but little about the small island. The Biblical significance of the island, hidden for centuries, was rediscovered in the 11th century. A Byzantine abbot, with imperial assistance, established a monumental fortress-like monastery, and dedicated it to the beloved Apostle. It wasn't until the 16th century that Western pilgrims came to visit sites hallowed by the presence of John. Recently, scholarly interest has centered around its famous library treasures." (Ibid., p. ii.)

*his feet. . . . His face was like the sun shining in
all its brilliance"* (1:12-13,16).

John collapsed at his feet, as though dead. But
then, he continues:

*". . . he placed his right hand on me and said: 'Do
not be afraid. I am the First and the Last. I am
the Living One; I was dead, and behold I am
alive for ever and ever! And I hold the keys of
death and Hades. Write, therefore, what you have
seen, what is now and what will take place later"*
(1:19).

I got a lump in my throat just thinking about
John scratching dictation on his parchment, as the
angel proclaimed the Word of the Lord. A parade of
images appeared, which must have left the disciple
aghast.

Then, if that weren't enough, suddenly the door of
heaven swung open, and John was invited to enter.
He saw bejeweled thrones, elders dressed in white,
lightning, blazing lamps, a crystal sea, living crea-
tures, angels, beasts, armies and — above all — the
Lamb of God.

He watched coming events unfold before his eyes:
horses and beasts engaging in battle, the first resurrection — ushering in the millennium, the great
judgment, the lake of fire. Finally, our friend saw the
glorious New Jerusalem. The Holy City, prepared for
God and His people.

*"Now the dwelling of God is with men, and he
will live with them. They will be his people, and
God himself will be with them and be their God.
He will wipe every tear from their eyes. There will
be no more death or mourning or crying or pain,*

for the old order of things has passed away"
(21:3-4).

What comfort this message must have brought to John, whose body had endured great persecution! Now it all made sense.

The closing words belong to Jesus. He begins with this compassionate invitation:

> *"I, Jesus, have sent my angel to give this testimony. . . . Whoever is thirsty, let him come; and whoever wishes, let him take the free gift of the water of life"* (22:17).

He then pauses to warn any who might attempt to add or subtract from the words dictated to John. To do so is to relinquish citizenship in the holy city.

Finally, our Lord offers these touching words of hope — words that John, and all of us who serve Him, long to hear: *"Yes, I am coming soon"* (v. 20).

Suddenly, I was jolted out of my deep thoughts by the monastery bells overhead, and the loud blast of our cruise ship. It was time to move on. To get on with life. I left that cave — but, somehow, John's cave left an indelible imprint on my mind and heart.

What an experience for the Apostle of love! John must have remained speechless for days. His mesmerized eyes, no doubt, continued to see flashbacks of that glorious panorama of scenes. Scenes that no mortal had ever been privileged to behold.

Why Not Me?

Without a doubt, we receive valuable perspective through **personal revelation**. Put simply, this refers to *times when God elects to disclose Himself (or His will) to whomever He chooses.*

It should not be surprising that the recipient of such a quintessential experience is referred to as a *"seer."*[3] Like John, the seer comes into direct contact with Deity, and is shown future events.

Go ahead, tell me which of your wishes you would most want God to grant? Fame? Inexhaustible funds? Peace on earth? The salvation of a friend? The last two would, no doubt, be very high on my list. But, also, it would be awesome to experience an authentic vision.

I must be honest. I've never experienced such an event. But, those who have seem to be revolutionized. The depth and quality of their perspective is expanded exponentially. They see clearer. In addition, they see rightly.

It would be great to simply be a bystander when *someone else* received a vision. I'd promise to be quiet — and just soak up some "warmed-over" inspiration.

I'm certain my sight would greatly improve. And I would share it with everyone. I can imagine myself describing it, in vivid detail, in a forthcoming book. (Wouldn't it have been nice to include in this chapter?)

---

3. "The **prophet** is (indeed) designated a **seer** (Heb. *hozeh*; LXX *horon*; 1 Chr. 21:9; 2 Chr. 9:29). The seer's visions, generally, have a twofold reference. On the one hand, they refer to the thing seen, the vision (*horama*) or the appearance of the vision (Exod. 3:3; Dan. 7:1). On the other hand, they show the effect on the seer. He is encouraged, chosen, shocked, pardoned (Gen. 15:1; Dan. 7:13). This prophetic vision involves, primarily, a revelation of God and His Word, and only then a visual impact: God lets it be known what he wants or what (H)e is going to do and 'shows' it to someone (i.e., seer) whom he has chosen for this purpose." (*Dictionary of New Testament Theology*, Colin Brown, ed., vol. 3, Grand Rapids: Zondervan, 1986, pp. 513-514.)

Authentic, heaven-inspired visions are repeatedly described in God's Word. Ones in the Old Testament focus, mainly, on Israel's fate and the coming of the greatly anticipated Messiah.

➤ **Isaiah's** vision revealed the fate of many nations, like Babylon, Moab, Syria, Egypt, etc. Also, he saw the ultimate deliverance of Israel. But, most important of all, the prophet was shown how the coming Messiah would be characterized (e.g., *"Branch from Jesse," "Prince of Peace," "Suffering Servant"*)

➤ **Ezekiel** opens his prophetic book with these words:
"In the thirtieth year, in the fourth month of the fifth day, while I was among the exiles by the Kebar River, the heavens opened and I saw visions of God" (Ezek. 1:1).

Ezekiel saw all sorts of strange things — like a flying wheel and dry bones. Again, all signs and symbols foretold of the eventual triumph of Israel and the appearing of our Savior.

➤ **Daniel** told a perplexed Nebuchadnezzar:
". . .there is a God in heaven who reveals mysteries. . .As for me, this mystery has been revealed" (Dan. 2:28,30).

His dream was interpreted, it came to pass as foretold, and the king began to praise God (4:34-37).

The prophet continued to have visions: of Belshazzar's death (Nebuchadnezzar's son), four beasts, ram and goat, a great war, end times and, again, the characteristics of the Messiah.

Visions didn't cease with Old Testament prophets.

Take a glance at this New Testament sampling:

> ➤ An angel of the Lord (Gabriel) appeared to **Zechariah**, as he was doing his stint as a temple priest. The startled, fearful man was told that John (the Baptist) would be born to his aged wife, Elizabeth. He doubted, and as a result, was made unable to speak until the birth took place (Luke 1:8-25).

> ➤ The same angel was sent to the small town of Nazareth. He appeared to a young teenage virgin, named **Mary**. She was told that she was *"highly favored"* to bear the Savior (Luke 1:26-38). Mary replied: *"May it be to me as you have said"* (v. 38).

> ➤ **Joseph** began what he thought was a peaceful night of sleep. The angel appeared and put his fears to rest: *"Joseph son of David, do not be afraid to take Mary home as your wife, because what is conceived in her is from the Holy Spirit. She will give birth to a son, and you are to give him the name Jesus, because he will save his people from their sins"* (Matt. 1:20b-21).

> ➤ On his roof, during prayertime, **Peter** became hungry. After falling into a trance, he saw heaven open and a large sheet — containing all kinds of non-kosher animals — coming to earth (Acts 10:9-23). A voice commanded: *"Get up, Peter. Kill and eat"* (v. 13). He resisted three times, calling them *"unclean."* The voice answered: *"Do not call anything impure that God has made clean"* (v. 15).

> What was the central message of this vision? Accept Gentiles with an open mind and heart — just as God has done. And, a few moments later

Peter had that opportunity. Cornelius, the centurion, and two of his friends were standing at his gate. *"Then Peter invited the men into the house to be his guests"* (v. 23).

➤ The Apostle **Paul** was blessed with visions. One occurred on the Damascus road, when he was en route to persecute Christians. *". . . suddenly a light from heaven flashed around him. He fell to the ground and heard a voice say to him . . . why do you persecute me?"* (Acts 9:4).

The event left him blinded for three days! This began Paul's conversion experience.

As he made his missionary journey, later, Paul had a nighttime vision of a man from Macedonia (Greece) standing and begging him, *"Come over to Macedonia and help us"* (Acts 16:9) He immediately departed for this land, *"concluding that God had called (him) to preach the gospel to them"* (v. 10).

As a rule, New Testament visions were quite specific. Rather than relating to Israel's salvation or triumph, or the Messiah's appearance (He was already with them), these visitations involved a particular, critical message to a selected person. Typically, it concerned one issue which usually had (and has) general implications.

We might conceive of such visions as parallel to God's sending "faxes from heaven." The instrument of delivery was none other than an angel of light. And, often, the imagery was quite spectacular: bright lights, booming voices, heaven's opening, vivid object lessons.

One thing is for certain: The message really came through. Dynamically. Emphatically. And the recipients received sight. And they were greatly impacted.

The Scriptures are emphatic in declaring: *"Where there is no vision the people perish"* (Prov. 29:18, KJV). This well-known verse is inscribed on government buildings in Washington D.C. Most misinterpret it to support an enlightenment theme, which claims that human reason can conquer all.

In actuality, the verse focuses on the kinds of visions depicted in this chapter. To paraphrase, the verse implies: Where, and in times when, God's personal revelation is not experienced, felt and acted upon by people, the resulting "spiritual drought" leads to calamity and chaos.[4]

Periodic revelation is essential for any people — whether it occurs in the present, or is a message from the past that has great relevance for the present (e.g., John's vision in Revelation).

Question: Is it crucial that we *all* experience visions? Not at all. But if we believe God keeps His promises, we can expect divine insight to sharpen our vision. God opens eyes (Eph. 1:18), gives wisdom

---

4. Proverbs 29:18 has been repeatedly misinterpreted to imply that an absence of an optimistic, creative, human dream — which transcends the present and mundane — sentences a people to failure and even anguish. The focus, here, is upon human ingenuity, foresight and futuristic imaging.

By contrast, the correct exegesis of the verse is rendered by the following commentaries:

"The law, the prophets and the wisdom literature meet in this verse. Where the revealed will of God, as expressed in His Word, is not kept constantly in view, his people break loose from their allegiance. The slave, like the son, will need proper training and discipline." (Earl C. Wolf, *Beacon Bible Commentary*, vol. 3, "Proverbs," Kansas City, MO: Beacon Hill, 1967.)

"(When) divine revelation, and the faithful preaching of

(James 1:5), and leads His children (Rom. 8:14). Collectively, Christians share the guidance and inspiration God gives. This way we all derive security, comfort, and assurance when we see more clearly!

A Brief Word of Caution

Another question: What about visions *since* Bible times? Are they reliable and helpful, or spurious and harmful?

Today, many claiming such "visitations" have received a wide range of reactions. Some are deemed insane, and their messages absurd; others are considered saintly, and their revelations crucial. Without a doubt, some appear to have more "credibility-wobble" than others.

The media repeatedly informs us about the most bizarre. Cult leaders declare irrational predictions and ultimatums. Misguided criminals attempt to legitimatize their heinous deeds, by claiming "*God told me.*" Evangelists give "clout" to monetary appeals, by passing on admonitions (and promising lucrative rewards) from heavenly beings.

---

the sacred testimonies are neither reverenced nor attended, the ruin of that land is at no great distance." (Adam Clarke, *Adam Clarke Commentary*, vol. 3, New York: Abingdon-Cokesbury, n.d.)

"Vision, rather 'revelation' (is connoted). The word denotes prophetic prediction, the revelation of God by His Seers (1 Sam. 9:9). The chief function of these (Seers) consisted of their watching over the vigorous fulfilling of the law, or in the enforcement of the claims of the law." (W. Harris, *The Preacher's Complete Homiletic Commentary*, "Proverbs," Grand Rapids: Baker Book House, 1986.)

Recently, there have been multiple sightings (apparitions) of the Virgin Mary — almost as many as of Elvis![5]

Just last month, someone in a nearby city invited news cameras to photograph a "very special" window

---

5. When on a study trip to Mexico, we were told that a peasant, Juan Diego, was honored by a personal appearance (apparition), and conversation with, the Virgin Mary. This occurred on a cold December day in 1531 — ten years after Spaniards conquered — near the hill of Tepeyac.

The message of Mary's was a directive in his native tongue: *"Go to the bishop of Mexico City and ask him to build a cathedral on this spot."*

The peasant ran to the bishop but was rebuffed. Why would the Mother of Jesus reveal herself to such a humble Indian?

Our friend returned to the place of the initial appearance, whereupon the Virgin told him to pick the roses from a bush (blooming in mid-winter) and take them to the bishop. After he collected the roses in his "tilma" (cloak), and opened it for the bishop, a magnificent color image of the Madonna — surrounded by a blazing solar corona, was imprinted on it.

The church was built. Today, the famous Our Lady of Guadalupe Basilica stands. The ancient cloth, now considered a miracle-inducing relic, hangs behind the main altar. So great is its power thought to be, tens of thousands of worshipers annually visit the site.

Scores crawl miles, on their bare knees (until bloody), to the church altar. Participants in this ritual are usually prompted by the anticipation of a special blessing, or, more likely, fear of an impending crisis.

Not only was this Indian peasant exalted and accepted by the Spanish, so were his people. Mexico, increasingly, became a body of united people — though class distinctions did remain. Roman Catholicism was declared to be the state religion.

"Our Lady of Guadalupe" (i.e., the dark-skinned Mary who appeared) was declared the Patron Saint of the Americas.

When the apparition took place, it was easy for the Indians to accept this new, revised version of their Aztec mother goddess, Tonantzin, thereby facilitating their conversion to Catholicism. Why?

pane — one that had "reflected the Blessed Virgin's image."

Thousands of ardent spectators huddled close by to see and touch. The traffic jam became so congested that the landlord removed the glass — and placed it

---

➤ They believed the apparition site to be a sacred hill, dedicated to Tonantzin. A temple to the latter stood where the first church was built.

➤ Also, there were striking similarities between Tonantzin and Guadalupe.

1. Tonantzin was associated with the moon and Guadalupe stands on a crescent moon.
2. Tonantzin, like Guadalupe, was seen as a nurturing, all-loving, "holy" mother.
3. Unlike traditional European images of the Virgin — she, like Tonantzin, stands alone (without the Christ Child). [But, unlike Tonantzin, she is pictured with the indigenous custom of a tassel, or maternity band, at her waist to indicate her pregnancy.]

Cf. *Los Angeles Times*, Dec. 11, 1995, "The Lady of Guadalupe Reaches Across Generations," p. E2.

✛ ✛ ✛ ✛ ✛

"Agoo, Philippines — Hundreds of thousands of pilgrims waited, wept and prayed Saturday under a blazing sun as they awaited an appearance by the Virgin Mary. Only a handful claimed they saw an apparition.

"Word of an expected apparition swept the Philippines, Asia's only predominantly Roman Catholic country, after a 12-year-old self-styled seer, Judiel Nieva, claimed to have seen the Virgin on the first Saturday of every month since 1989.

"Nieva's family owns an image of Mary, which was said to have shed tears of blood last month. Residents of Agoo (population 42,000) claim Nieva is a seer and that communion wafers and wine turn to flesh and blood in his mouth.

"The Roman Catholic hierarchy has reacted cautiously to the claims. (Judgment is withheld pending an investigation.) Belief in apparitions associated . . . runs deep in Philippine culture." (*Los Angeles Times*, Associated Press item, Mar. 7, 1993, p. A11.

in a warehouse. Someone immediately offered him $200 for the relic.[6]

Was the sighting legitimate? Were the persons involved sincere? Furthermore, were people spiritually awakened or irreparably damaged, by this event? It is not my place, nor purpose, to pass judgment. I am only stating that a great many vision claims are made daily.

One final question: Should we equip ourselves to discern the veracity of such claims?[7] The answer is,

---

6. "The blurry kitchen window that many believe bore a heaven-sent silhouette of the Virgin Mary has been put into storage. . . . William R. Derrick Associates, managers of the S. Oxnard apartment where the image was first discovered Monday, reclaimed the pane of glass Friday morning.

"'We didn't want anyone selling it or profiting from the incident,' said property manager Iris Wilson. 'It's time for this to stop. It serves no purpose to have this continue.'

"Hundreds of believers and curious alike flocked to the modest neighborhood where the image was seen. The property managers ordered the window removed. . .after someone shot into the crowd Tuesday night, slightly injuring two people.

"The owner of the Oxnard glass shop that removed the window put it on display and offered to sell it to the highest bidder.

"Shop owner said he received a $200 offer. . .angering residents who believed that Rizzie planned to profit from a blessed event. Rizzie said Friday he planned all along to donate the money to a church.

"'I don't want no more of this,' Rizzie said. 'I'm not going to be the bad guy no more.'

"Wilson said the kitchen window will remain hidden indefinitely. (Fred Alvarez, *Thousand Oaks News Chronicle*, Dec. 12, 1992, p. B2.)

7. In his classic book, *Impressions*, Martin Wells Knapp explains that impressions (i.e., visions) originate from three sources: above (from God), below (from Satan), inside (from ourselves). The danger occurs, according to the author, when impressions from below and inside are ascribed to God (Cincinnati: Revivalist Pub.,1892).

obviously, affirmative. Paul declares to the Philippian church:

> "*And this is my prayer: that your love may abound more and more in knowledge and depth of insight, so that **you may be able to discern what is best** and may be pure and blameless until the day of Christ*" (Phil. 1:9-10, emphasis added).

In our day of demagogues and charlatans, it's quite all right to be a tad skeptical when hearing someone boast of a special revelation from God. Especially, when that person claims that the message has implications for us (e.g., "*God told me to tell you to marry me.*")!

In distinguishing divine guidance/visions/leading that is legitimate from what is questionable, we must rely on spiritual enlightenment of God's Spirit. Jesus said: "*But when he, the Spirit of truth, comes, he will guide you into all truth*" (John 16:13).

However, in the process of seeking such direction, it may be helpful to have a checklist. Here are some pertinent questions that might sharpen our discernment regarding vision claims:

- Is the message consistent with scriptural teaching? (Heb. 4:12)
- Is the alleged directive, or interpretation, consistent with the general character and purposes of God? (Ps. 111; Eph. 5:1a)
- Is the vision consistent with what the church as Christ's body has known and believed? (1 Cor. 14:33)
- Does the message focus on personal gain or servanthood? (Matt. 20:26)
- Do authentic Christians seem to be in agreement with the thrust of the message? (Matt. 18:19)

Instances of divine guidance can be extremely valuable sources of perspective. We gain sight from them — directly and indirectly.

But, there is a second important source of perspective. One that is, no doubt, much more familiar to most of us. In contrast to personal revelation, this one is continuously present in our daily lives — that is, if we are blessed with healthy, normal, physical capacities.

Let's explore it.

A Pause to Reflect

Before proceeding, let's ask ourselves a few questions. Questions that will help us to summarize, and understand, what we have just read.

1. **How do I feel about the personal revelations or divine guidance that others have received? Am I skeptical? Impressed? Jealous?**

2. **Have I ever experienced a "special visitation" (vision, voice, overpowering impression, etc.) from God — or one of His agents? If so, how did it impact my life immediately after it occurred? After a period of time? If not, how do I think I might have responded? Would I be a better person?**

3. If I could speak directly to John, what would I ask him? (Take the time to write the questions. Then, state why you would ask these specific ones. If you choose, you might guess what his answers might be.)

CHAPTER SEVEN

Perception:

Consulting the Ultimate Optometrist

*"Only in quiet waters things mirror themselves undistorted.
Only in a quiet mind is adequate perception of the world."*
(Hans Margolius)

*"The farther back you can look,
the farther forward you are likely to see."*
(Winston Churchill)

"See everything. Overlook a great deal. Correct a little."
(Pope John XXIII)

Our heavenly Father provides a second means of attaining perspective. In contrast to personal revelation, it is available to most of us. This incredible capacity is **perception** — *the ability "to become aware of phenomena directly, by means of our senses."*[1]

Without diminishing the importance of all five senses, our primary focus is on our "eyegate to the world." During waking hours, our eyes perceive the

---

1. "Perception . . . involve(s) more than passively registering the stimuli that impinge upon our senses. Our current expectations and our prior experiences influence what we perceive and how we interpret it." (H. Andrew Michener, *Social Psychology*, second edition. San Diego: Harcourt Brace Javanovick, Publisher, 1992, p. 117.)

world continuously. Our minds, then, take what is seen and process it in a beautiful and complex manner.

Do our eyes sometimes deceive us, causing us to channel false information into our minds? Who would deny it? Sight distortion is as common as lightning bugs on a July evening in Tennessee.[2]

One person put it bluntly, but correctly: "At times, all of us are a lot like ink blotters. We soak it all up, but (then) we get it all backwards!"

And our misperceptions have implications. Sometimes, they prompt us to indulge in hearty, therapeutic laughter.

Umbrellas to Snare and to Spare

It seems as though popular speaker-author, Tony Campolo, had an "umbrella problem." He lost them. His wife suggested that he devote an entire day searching for the ones he had misplaced. He said, "Fine. I'll do it tomorrow."

Now Tony customarily rode the train to his teaching assignment at Eastern College. This morning was no exception — nor was the weather. It was raining buckets! As he jumped on, he placed his umbrella on the seat.

On approaching his stop, he nonchalantly reached for the wrong umbrella, and heard a woman's voice exclaim, "Sir, pardon me, but that's *my* umbrella!"

---

2. ". . . everyday . . . perception . . . work(s) fairly well . . . accurate enough to permit (reliable conclusions). (But) . . . perception . . . can be unreliable. Even a skilled observer can misperceive, misjudge, and reach the wrong conclusions. Once we form a wrong impression, we are likely to persist in our misperceptions and misjudgments." (Ibid.)

Tony sheepishly apologized, then disembarked at his destination.

That day, he located an incredible number of lost umbrellas. And, sure enough, all were legitimately his. At the end of the day, he grabbed his satchel and the umbrellas.

As he boarded the train, and started to sit down, he glanced up and couldn't believe his eyes. There she was — the same lady whose umbrella he had almost taken that morning.

Looking at his armload of umbrellas, and with a wry smile, she said, "Sir, I see that you've had a very profitable day!"

Tony's initial reaction was to offer a convincing explanation. But, he wisely thought better of it. A nod and a smile had to suffice.

Some misperceptions, like this one, break a smile. But, others can break a heart. Treasured relationships can end up strained or even severed.

At one time or another, we've all been victimized. Furthermore, we can attest to the intense discomfort — mental, physical, even spiritual — that lingers in its wake.

This Money Tree Had Thorns

A good friend of mine, Andy, was a respected Sunday School teacher of young couples. He and his wife, Shirley, had built the class to over ninety persons.

Then, he graduated from Western Evangelical Seminary — en route to his life-goal of becoming a minister. He applied for a church, went for the interview, and eagerly accepted the assignment.

The next Sunday, the decision was announced to

the class. Admittedly, both he and they, felt conflicting emotions: The assignment seemed very promising, but the separation was most likely to be painful!

To express their love and goodwill, the class planned a farewell party at Silver Creek Falls — an isolated park some distance from the city. It would follow the morning service of Andy and Shirley's last Sunday. Everyone seemed very enthusiastic.

The big day arrived. Immediately after the worship service, the honorees rushed home to change into casual clothes. The plan was to be at the park by 1:30 p.m. No problem anticipated. After all, it was only fifteen miles east of town.

They arranged to meet another couple (Mike and Bobbi) at the edge of town. Andy pulled up at the designated corner. Soon thereafter, the other couple arrived. Their daughter let them out and drove away.

They walked over to Andy's parked car. It was obvious that Mike was carrying a farewell present, shaped like a large picture. Andy suggested that he put it in the trunk, and threw him his car keys. Mike placed his gift inside, pushed down the trunk lid, got into the car, and said "Let's go."

Andy retorted, "Let's go where? Give me the car keys." Mike responded, with a troubled countenance, "What car keys?" Andy: "The car keys I gave you to open the trunk!" Mike panicked: "You're not going to believe this, but I've locked your keys in the trunk."

Andy quickly turned to Shirley for the extra set she always carried. Unfortunately, this time, she had left them on the dresser.

The two men walked over a mile to the nearest telephone. They called a locksmith, who came, but was unable to get the trunk open. While there, Mike attempted to phone his daughter, but she wasn't home. Andy looked at his watch. It was already 2:30! He anguished.

Some "avowed car experts" stopped and offered assistance. They would solve the problem in a few minutes. Their solution? Take out the back seat. They tried — unsuccessfully.

Finally, after repeated calls, Mike's daughter was reached and returned to where the four were stranded. She took them back to Andy's house.

He borrowed a neighbor's ladder, climbed on the roof, and pried open the bedroom window. The keys were finally retrieved. All got back into the car and headed for the park. They arrived at around five o'clock.

There were only two couples left. One stared at Andy and Shirley with an "it-takes-a-lot-of-nerve" look in their eyes.

Andy stammered out an explanation: "I can tell that you don't understand. It honestly wasn't our fault. We locked our keys in the trunk."

The husband of one of the remaining couples responded: "Yea. Sure. Just tell me, I'm curious: How did you do on the front nine?" [a snide insinuation that the tardy couples had been playing golf.]

His wife flippantly added: "Your gifts, and the money tree we made for you, are over there (pointing). Go ahead and take them with you. We have to leave, or we'll be late for the evening church service."

According to Andy and Shirley, this event was extremely traumatic. Granted, eventually, the class understood (thanks to Mike and Bobbi's advocacy), but it was never quite the same. A residue of resentment remained.

The misperception had, indeed, led to misjudgment. And it didn't cease there. Misjudgment prompted mistreatment. Judge, prosecutor, jury and executioner became one and the same.

To repeat, as is so often the case in all of our lives, the downward spiral went like this:

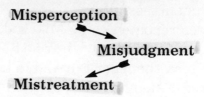

Misperception

Misjudgment

Mistreatment

What about the whole issue of perception? Can our senses be relied upon to provide trustworthy perspective? Let's explore this issue.

Slivers, Logs and Other Eye Pollutants

It is foolish to discredit the immense value, and incredible complexity, of our senses. Any scientist worth his salt marvels at their precision and intricacy. The Psalmist struck a resounding note of truth, when praying: *"Thank you for making me so wonderfully complex! It is amazing to think about. Your workmanship is marvelous — and how well I know it"* (139:14 LB).

But, we must not be naïve regarding inherent weaknesses of our natural equipment. Case in point: the eyes. Undeniably, we're prone to visual misperception. It's little wonder that courts insist on multiple witnesses, research studies employ numerous, independent observers, and everyone seems to be relying on video cameras.

Introductory psychology texts present pictures that illustrate humankind's propensity to visual illusion.

In one instance, the reader is requested to cover

one eye, and count the picture's cubes. The same is requested for the other eye. The totals are remarkably inconsistent.

On other occasions, social psychological experimenters have interrupted large groups of people with mock disturbances, fights, spurious warnings of calamity, etc.

Immediately afterwards, those present were asked to describe what they saw. There was a wide range of disagreement as to: who perpetrated the interruption; what was the physical position of the participants; and, what actually occurred. Even more amazing, most were very adamant concerning the accuracy of their report!

Thus, as we can see, there are natural tendencies that prompt us to have skewed vision. The result is an incorrect, faulty perspective.

Here are a few of such unfortunate tendencies:

1. Due to fear, or anticipated pain, we refuse to have a good, thorough look. We either fail to see at all, or have only a glimpse. In both cases, our report is based on what we think we saw (or might have seen). One author rightly declares: "The most painful act that human(s) can perform is seeing." He continues: (But) it is (only) in that act of seeing that (accuracy comes and) love is born."[3]

2. We see with selective attention. Our eyes gravitate toward object, places and people of particular interest. That's why, in church congregations, we're often blind (hence, insensitive and unrespon-

---

3. Anthony De Mello, *The Way to Love: The Last Meditations of Anthony De Mello* (New York: Doubleday, 1991), front book cover.

sive) to those with lackluster countenance, attire or personality. Is it any wonder that we fail to pick up, visually, their subtle "cries for help?" We're too occupied with gazing at people that we consider to be impressive (cf. James 2:2-9).

3. Our eyes can be deceived by those who disguise their true intentions. A radio commentator once told about a man who pulled his car into a "Handicap" space at a fast-food restaurant. He got out and hobbled toward the entrance. As he opened the door to the restaurant, he glanced back at his car and noticed an intruder reaching into the window of his car, stealing his "Handicapped Person" sign.

This "physically challenged" man sprinted across the parking lot, made a "shoestring tackle" that would have impressed any N.F.L. coach, muscled the thief to the ground, and wrested back his sign — forgetting that he had exposed his hypocrisy to all who observed.

Things aren't always what they seem! As God's Word proclaims: "*. . . now (we) know in part . . .*" (1 Cor. 13:12b).

4. We possess distortions. Some window panes are referred to as "opaque." These are impervious to the complete passage of light. Result: When trying to look through them we get a fictitious perspective. "*We see through a glass darkly*" (1 Cor. 13:12a KJV).

At times, the problem is with the "window" — it is smudgy. But perhaps more frequently the difficulty lies in our vision. It is obvious that the couples at our friends' farewell party had "jaundiced eyes." What seemed to be true to them, wasn't.

With these maladies in mind, is there any wonder that illusion doggedly persists? That even eyewitness accounts are frequently proven unreliable?

Furthermore, need we question why God's Word repeatedly commands us to refrain from judging others? In His time-honored discourse on a Galilean mountain, our Lord emphatically declared: *"Do not judge . . ."* (Matt. 7:1). Exclamation point!

Proceeding with Extreme Caution

Fully realizing our propensities toward misperception, what attitudes are we well-advised to possess? Here are a few:

1. Be humbly tentative. Life's final curtain hasn't been lowered. That "size-challenged" lady hasn't sung the final number! People and situations often change. God has a wonderful way of recycling. Things can change for the better — and we can, too. Especially our eyesight!

2. Insist on multiple sightings. When attempting to pinpoint a forest fire, rangers use the method of *triangulation*. All nearby towers are requested to calculate the direction and distance of the smoke — from their respective positions. Then, after all angles are carefully computed, the fire's position is precisely located.

Similarly, before drawing incriminating conclusions about others, we're wise to observe them from a multiplicity of vantage points. One suspicious-looking instance, as a rule, should not outweigh an impressive record of goodness. Love believes the best — until, of course, irrefutable, triangulated evidence is forthcoming. But, even then, we are to continue loving.

3. Commit to prayerful obedience. Picking up on the previous point, it is our reaction to what we think we've seen, that verifies the depth of our spirituality. We must await "God's green light," before responding. To pounce upon others, without such direction from our merciful Lord, and with only suspicions, is to act foolishly and to annihilate relationships.

In summary, our eyes were not created to be "squinty in judging." We are biblically-admonished to use them for a far more noble purpose.

4. Above all, we must fix our eyes on Jesus.

Let's allow Eugene Peterson's poetic paraphrase of Hebrews 12:2-3 speak to our hearts:

> Keep your eyes on Jesus, who both began and finished the race we're in. Study how he did it. Because he never lost sight of where he was headed — that exhilarating finish in and with God — he could put up with anything along the way: cross, shame, whatever.
>
> And now he's there, in the place of honor right alongside God. When you find yourself flagging in your faith, go over that story again, item by item, that long litany of hostility he plowed through. That will shoot adrenaline into your souls.[4]

In spite of our constant penchant for distraction, we must focus on Him. To do so is to dramatically improve our insight, foresight, and our hindsight. And what will that lead to?

Knowledge is one derivative. But, coupled with this is something even more valuable: we will receive wisdom — for He is its Author! Hear the Writer of Proverbs: *"For the Lord gives wisdom, and from his mouth come knowledge and understanding"* (Prov. 2:6) Similarly, Paul declares: *". . . that they may*

---

4. Eugene Peterson, *The Message* (Colorado Springs: NavPress, 1994), p. 559.

know the mystery of God, namely, Christ, in whom are hidden all the treasures of wisdom and knowledge" (Col. 2:2-3; cf. Jer. 10:12).

I once heard about a child-prodigy violinist, who riveted her eyes on a place in the concert hall's balcony, as she performed a flawless recital. The pint-sized virtuoso was encountered after the concert, and asked: "What were you looking at?" Her answer was immediate: "I was gazing at my teacher, who was up there directing every note I played."

In life's concert, which we all play, let's fix our eyes on the loving countenance of our Savior. The One who orchestrates us through our brightest joys, and darkest trials, with precision and compassion.

And where can we see our Lord? Many places.

> In the eyes of His obedient **followers** — His saints. We must take the time to seek them out, whether it be personally or on printed page. (cf. Heb. 10:25)

> In the marvelous magnitude of His glorious **universe.** How long has it been since we've witnessed the incredible beauty of a butterfly or sunset? (cf. Ps. 148)

> Finally, we see Him in His inspirational **teachings.** In His rich parables. His wise answers to friendly, and antagonistic, questions. And, especially, in His revolutionary Sermon on the Mount.

To see Jesus, really see Him, begins a wonderful chain reaction. We will find ourselves drawn to Him — following Him more nearly, and loving Him more dearly. Day by day.

All of this adds up to a more accurate and focused perspective. One that, someday, we can take to "heaven's bank!"

But, What About The Other Guy?

Unfortunately, improving our perception doesn't guarantee that we will avoid getting stuck. Others, with whom we must relate, can adamantly cling to their blurry and distorted vision. As a result, our potential for happiness can be checkmated.

Typically, we rack our brain, trying to figure what's driving our antagonists — asking ourselves such questions as:

> ➤ Do we possibly look like someone who once did them dirty?

> ➤ Could their attitude be generated by feelings of jealousy or envy?

> ➤ Or, is it based on an inability to control us, or use us for their purposes?

No answer satisfies us. Result: We remain restless, and incapable of generating any plan to resolve our quandary. No scheme for reforming those who are insistent on "raining on our parade."

Question: What should we do when such "irregular persons" choose to misperceive, misjudge and mistreat us?[5] And when, deep down, we know it's positively not our fault?

Not a snap question. One that we'll attempt to

---

5. Cf. Jon Johnston, *Walls or Bridges: How to Build Relationships That Glorify God* (Grand Rapids: Baker Book House, 1988).

The author enumerates the characteristics of "irregular people" (based on material from Joyce Landorf, *Irregular People*. Waco, TX: Word Books, 1982) as:

   1) are selectively blind;
   2) make biased comparisons;
   3) have emotional deafness;
   4) possess communication problems;
   5) are easily offended.

offer an answer to in our next chapter. It all has to do with our bottom-line point of view. Let's zero in on this crucial topic, but not before we stop to reflect on what we've discussed.

A Moment's Reflection

1. Was there a time when I was misperceived (or I misperceived someone). Was it amusing? What valuable lessons were learned?

2. What instance can I think of when misperception led to misjudgment — and misjudgment resulted in mistreatment? In the life of a biblical character. In the life of someone I directly know or heard about.

3. Did I ever have a misperception that was eventually cleared up? What brought about the correction in my sight? How did that incident improve my perspective today?

He goes on to offer a taxonomy of such troublemakers. The types are:
    1) regular irregulars (persons with deficient upbringing);
    2) personality-defect irregulars (serious misfits in society);
    3) sociopathic irregulars (have no feeling);
    4) mental irregulars (genetic or stress-related cognitive difficulty) (pp. 108-114).

CHAPTER EIGHT

Point of View:

Exchanging Faded Cardboard for Polished Mahogany

*"The clearsighted do not rule the world,
but they sustain and console it."*
(Agnes Repplier)

*"You see things that are, and say 'why?';
I dream things that never were and say 'why not?'"*
(George Bernard Shaw)

*"One can never have the correct viewpoint without,
first of all, having the right viewing point."*
(Larry Keene)

My doctor friend, Gary, had a car accident not long ago. Gawkers quickly converged. He jumped out, and loudly proclaimed: "I'm the luckiest man alive! Look at me. Not even a scratch. And besides that, I just renewed my insurance two days ago!"

In amazement, the people gazed at his demolished vehicle, then at him. We've all seen that look — the kind that seriously questions a person's sanity. Surely, only some kind of a nut would be upbeat at a time like this.

It was a clear case of contrasting points of view. Gary placed the event on the backdrop of God's good, providential care. The onlookers stood there shaking their heads, pitying this poor fellow who had been "snakebitten by adversity."

What's more, they knew that his positive viewpoint was certain to vanish — just as soon as he recovered from the shock.

The third source of perspective, one that will be our primary focus throughout the remainder of this book, is **point of view**. Put simply, it is the *mental framework with which we process all incoming information and experience*. The slant. The spin. The interpretation we give to everything we consciously encounter.

In the words of one psychologist, "We use concept(ual) (frameworks) to encode stimuli and make sense of them."[1] To illustrate, we interpret the following according to our unique point of view:

➤ sounds — as noise or music;

➤ smells — as sewage or perfume;

➤ pressures against our skin — as pinches or kisses;

➤ words — as insults or compliments.

The preceding chapters describe two important "delivery systems" for formulating our perspective: personal revelation and perception. The benefits and limitations of each were described. Let's briefly summarize.

---

1. H. Andrew Michener, *Social Psychology*, Second Edition (San Diego: Harcourt Brace Javanovich, Publishers, 1992), pp. 117-119.

When a perceiver groups together certain stimulus objects, and excludes others, he is said to have a *"concept."* When concepts are organized into related clusters, they become *"schemas."* Schemas serve three important functions:

1) guide what we perceive in our environment and how we interpret it;
2) organize information in memory, thus, affect what we remember and forget;
3) guide inferences and judgments about people and things.

Personal revelation yields inspiration and helpful guidance. Typically, however, most of us receive such Divine messages secondhand. We only hear about them. Thus, we have the challenging task of deciphering which are reliable, and what specific messages are applicable to us.

By contrast, perception is universally experienced. The up side is that most of us are born with the marvelous capacity to see. Unfortunately, it is equally true that we are very prone to perception error. Plain and simple, our eyes often play tricks on us.

How about point of view? Unlike personal revelation, it is generated by our own minds — not by a spectacular "visitation." Unlike perception, it's not restricted to the actual process of seeing; rather, it contextualizes and provides interpretation for what is seen.[2]

Bottom line: Point of view offers us the greatest potential for perspective improvement. The kind of improvement that will help us cope with nagging, stressful relationship impasses. The kind in which we are victimized — unfairly misperceived, misjudged, mistreated.

To understand its rich potential, let's lean in a little closer to examine its essential features.

Nuts-and-Bolts of our Point of View

First, our point of view does not emerge by happenstance. Rather, it is crafted by design — piece by

---

2. Although we speak of personal revelation, perception and point of view as though they were separate entities, it should be understood that they often overlap.

To illustrate, the apostle John perceived his vision. Likewise, after the "visitation" experience, his point of view was forever altered.

piece. Important influences impact the viewpoint we lock onto. What are some of these influences?

1. Persons we consider to be like ourselves.

We're ingrained by an overpowering "consciousness of kind." This term, originated by sociologist W.I. Thomas, implies that we closely identify with certain significant others (e.g., lovers, family, job associates, church or club companions).[3] Such consciousness draws us to their point of view. In short, we indulge in "group-think."

As a result, our opinions become about as predictable as traffic during L.A.'s rush hours. Just ask advertisers or politicians. In most instances, all that's necessary to know what we think, is to learn what people closest to us think. We line up in cadence, like soldiers awaiting our orders.[4]

How long has it been since we've heard about a NRA member pleading for rigid gun control, or an Ivy League biology professor clamoring for creationism to be taught in public schools? Slim chance in both cases!

To reiterate: our viewpoint usually slips into alignment with that of "our kind of people."

2. Tradition.

Grab a pencil and fill in the following blanks:

"as hungry as a _____"; "as wise as an _____"; "as quiet as a _____."

No doubt, 99% of us automatically answered wolf,

---

3. W.I. Thomas and Florian Znaniecki, *The Polish Peasant in Europe and America*, Vol. 1 (New York: Alfred A. Knopf, 1927).

4. I'm reminded of Fabre's caterpillars, who formed a ring on the edge of a flowerpot. Each followed the one ahead for seven days and nights, until starvation and exhaustion caused them to die and fall. (Ted Engstrom, *The Fine Art of Friendship*. Nashville: Thomas Nelson Publishers, 1985).

owl and mouse. Why? Because we've heard these phrases repeated since we were cradle bound.

Try this one:

How should "ghiti" be pronounced? _____

Go ahead, give it a shot. The answer is "FISH" — that is, if we pronounce "gh" like in "laugh," and "iti" as we do in "ambition." Then, why do we refrain from pronouncing "ghiti" like "fish?" That's a no-brainer. The obvious answer: tradition.

Like word usage, our point of view is greatly impacted by tradition. December 25 is not just another day. A person who waves is amiably responded to. Everybody knows what to do when approaching a stop sign.

And kids? We consider them mischievous but lovable. I came across this description of a "little guy" some time ago. (Just as endearing a piece could have been written on "little girls.") As we read it, let's allow faces and names to come to mind.

A BOY

After a male baby has grown out of triangles and has acquired pants, freckles and so much dirt that relatives do not dare to kiss it between meals, it becomes a BOY.

A boy can swim like a fish, run like a deer, climb like a squirrel, bellow like a calf, can eat like a pig and balk like a mule.

He's a piece of skin stretched over an appetite. A noise covered with smudges.

Why does he seem like a tornado? Because he comes at the most unexpected times, hits the most unexpected places, and leaves everything a wreck behind him. He is a growing animal that must be fed, watered, and kept warm.

A boy is useful in running an errand — with only the help of five or six adults. The zest with which a little guy does one is equaled only by the speed of a turtle on a hot July day.

He's a natural spectator. He watches parades, fires, ballgames, cars, boats and airplanes with equal fervor — but won't watch a clock to know when it's time for dinner.

A boy will faithfully imitate his dad, in spite of all efforts to teach him good manners.

A boy, if not washed too often and kept in a cool quiet place after each accident, will survive broken bones, hornets, swimming holes, fights and nine helpings of pie.

A boy is a superlative promise, a periodic nuisance, the problem of our times, a joy forever, the hope of our nation — all combined.

In the final essence, a boy is what his parents help him to become. He's proof positive that God hasn't yet given up on mankind![5]

Traditional points of view provide security, links with the past, feelings of intimacy and a host of other benefits. Unfortunately, they can gear us toward thinking in time-worn, futile manners, so that we continue to repeat mistakes of the past.

3. Early life experiences.

University of Pennsylvania social psychologist, Martin Seligman, declares that all of us have either a basic *optimistic* or *pessimistic* viewpoint. Furthermore, we disclose it through our "explanatory style."

In his ten-year study, he concluded that the crucial test occurs when we are faced with hardship. In short, when we're stuck. Our attempts to explain our misfor-

---

5. Source unknown, but shared with me by my former colleague, Dr. Bob Gilliam.

tune follow a pattern, and we have two major options.

If we tend to see our hardship as *internal, stable* and *global* (i.e., feel we're at fault, it will last forever, and it will undermine all we do), we are pessimists to the core.[6]

By contrast, if we feel our misfortune is *external, unstable* and *specific* (i.e., we've been victimized, it's going away quickly, and it involves this one situation only), we're optimists.

See summary chart below. Then, if you care to take a brief test that reveals your "optimism-pessimism quotient," refer to Appendix B.

1st INTERNAL or EXTERNAL
(Either we feel that we're the cause, or we explain it by referring to other people or circumstances.)

2nd STABLE or UNSTABLE
(Either we think that we're locked into the situation permanently, or that it's something that is transitional.)

3rd GLOBAL or SPECIFIC
(Either we believe that our trial will undermine everything, or that it is confined to a particular situation.)

---

6. In a November, 1995, Convocation at Pepperdine University, author, psychologist, and alumnus, Richard Carlson, spoke on the effects of negative thinking. His research concluded that, in the course of each 24-hour day, (on an average) every person has one hundred *"thought-attacks."* He defined the latter as "intruding, negative thoughts that have the potential of inflicting our mind and life." To counter them, we need to improve our "emotional quotient," or train our minds to minimize their influence. (*You Can Be Happy No Matter What.* San Rafael, CA: New World Library, 1992).

So what's the big deal? Why does it matter whether we have an optimistic or pessimistic point of view? Well, check out the researchers' findings:

> **Depression:** If children start life pessimistic, they inevitably become depressed. But, if they begin life depressed (and later became optimistic), they overcome depression.

> **Achievement:** Optimistic college freshmen (measured by the "Attributional Style Test") receive higher grades than expected; but for pessimistic students, it's the opposite.

> **Physical Health:** Starting at age 45 and extending into the mid-60s, optimists have remarkably fewer chronic illnesses commonly associated with middle age.

Question: If optimism/pessimism is such a deeply-entrenched point of view, with crucial consequences, what are its sources? According to Seligman, there are three: our mother's viewpoint (depressed or upbeat); the "criticism style" of our grammar school teachers (harsh or reinforcing); and, the reality of our first major childhood event (positive or devastating).[7]

With this in mind, who could possibly deny the importance of early childhood? It, along with people who are close and traditions, have a great influence on our viewpoint.

Second, but in spite of these influences, we have the ultimate control over our point of view. We still choose the slant that we give to everything that impacts us.

Ask Viktor Frankl, whose classic *In Search for Meaning* describes how his point of view helped him

---

7. Taken from video entitled "Discovering Psychology: Motivation and Emotion," narrated by Phillip Zimbardo, social psychologist at Stanford University.

survive a Nazi prison camp. He intentionally injected meaning into this excruciating experience. Result: He not only survived, he thrived. Others who lacked this ability perished.[8]

Ask lottery winners. Studies disclose that many fail to cope with their millions. Surprisingly, sudden wealth often yields sudden trauma: relationship crises (e.g., divorce), serious psychological problems, and even crime.

Why? Many choose an unhealthy, counterproductive point of view. One that discounts pre-millionaire values they once cherished (e.g., hard work, respect for others, humility), and opt for ones that insure misery and failure (e.g., greed, elitism, materialism).

But for both Frankl and the decadent "big spin" winners, the choice of a point of view was theirs to make. And, once again, that choice was crucial. It always is!

Here's the good news: Our point of view, once chosen, can be discarded in favor of a better one.

Psychologist Harry Stack Sullivan employs the imagery of a framed picture. Most of us recall finding an old, treasured photograph in our attic. Its frame, more often than not, is a faded, water-stained, piece of cardboard.

We may have taken it for reframing, and the same, unaltered picture comes back to us in an exquisite, mahogany or oak frame. The results are astounding. The picture takes on an incredible beauty — all because of the new frame!

Dr. Sullivan, a therapist, discovered that many of his clients saw themselves as powerless to change the

---

8. Viktor Frankl, *Man's Search for Meaning: An Introduction to Logotherapy* (New York: Washington Square Press, Inc., 1963).

basic "picture" of their lives. They seemed boxed-in, derailed, stuck in painful, defeating circumstances. And the thought of this made them feel hopeless and helpless.

He simply suggested that they "exchange their frame." That they adopt a new set of attitudes and visualizations to contextualize their situation. So that they might be more at peace.

It happened. Even though the circumstances, within their photo, didn't instantly improve, they found life much more bearable. Lessons were learned. Self-improvement was initiated. Understanding was expanded. Forgiveness was granted. And, to their surprise, often things eventually got better.[9]

Point of view. It really counts for a lot when it comes to our overall perspective. It can become our psychological shock absorber. Our corrective lens. Our survival kit. The means of recasting reality, so that we're no longer punished by adversity. Or, for that matter, no longer tripped up by successes.

My friend puts it in a nutshell: Adopting the right point of view removes the wobble in our lives — or, at the very least, it makes that wobble much more bearable!

---

9. Harry Stack Sullivan offers an excellent example of "reframing." After one of his patients poured out disclosures of multiple phobias, and indulged in self-pity, he declared to her: "Ma'am, try saying this to yourself: I must have a remarkably strong constitution to possess as many mental illnesses as I do and still be surviving. Someone with a weak constitution would have given up long ago!" The lady thought about his words a moment, smiled, perked-up and said: "I guess you're right. I am pretty special after all!" She departed with a joyful countenance." (cf. Salvador Minuchin, *Families in Family Therapy*, Cambridge: Harvard University Press, 1974).

We've all encountered persons with inspiring, unique, humorous and productive points of view. Help me turn the pages as I share some "unframed" pictures in my scrapbook. Some points of view that I've collected through the years, that have enriched my life.

But before we charge ahead full steam, let's pause to reflect a bit.

Time Out

1. Can I think of an instance when someone else's point of view contrasted sharply with mine? (refer to Gary's car accident) Did I attempt to see things from the other vantage point, or did I reject the other point of view immediately — and carte blanche?

2. To what extent do I mimic the point of view of my parents or friends? Why do I feel this need to conform (or feel freedom to not conform)? What does this say about me?

3. Referring to Martin Seligman's "optimism-pessimism" model, which one do I most gravitate toward when facing hardship? How could this relate to any depression I might feel, my ability to work above my potential, and my health?

CHAPTER NINE

Snapshots of Favorite Viewpoints

"We don't see the world as it is, we see it as we are."
(Anaïs Nin)
"A romantic sees life through rose-colored glasses;
but a realist doesn't need corrective lenses."
(Source Unknown)
"Things work out best for those who make the best
of the way that things work out"
(Art Linkletter)

People around us are pretty quick to tell us where they're coming from. In short, we're bombarded by many points of view on a daily basis. Most fail to inspire, or even interest, us. They capture our imagination about as much as a plate of cold spaghetti with coagulated tomato sauce.

There are others that, with certainty, mesmerize our minds and hearts. To interface with them is to have an "aha experience." Lights go on, vision clears, the heart is warmed, the mind is activated. And, indeed, sometimes we can be motivated to get unstuck.

Through the years, I have clipped some viewpoints that have seemed especially significant. Some motivated me to think. Others to feel deeply. Still others to smile or laugh. Allow me to share my sampling.

Sign Language

Signs declare points of view, whether blatant, subtle or in-between. Whether the Burma Shave kind of the '40s, or the controversial Joe Camel brand of today.

James Dobson collects humorous ones. His favorites include:

(on an office door:)

```
NO ADMITTANCE;
ADMITTANCE BY APPOINTMENTS;
NO APPOINTMENTS
```

(in the backwoods of the south:)

```
I DIP SNUFF.
IF YOU WON'T BLOW SMOKE IN MY FACE,
I WON'T SPIT IN YOURS
```

(on the fence of a monastery in Santa Monica:)

```
ABSOLUTELY NO TRESPASSING.
TRESPASSERS WILL BE PROSECUTED
TO THE FULLEST EXTENT OF THE LAW
—The Sisters of Mercy
```

(at the entrance of a restaurant:)

```
NO DOGS ALLOWED EXCEPT SEEING EYE DOGS
```

[question:] Who will read it? The dog can't, and neither can the blind person!

(on the wall of a post office:)

```
IT IS A FEDERAL OFFENSE TO
ASSAULT AN EMPLOYEE {while on duty}
```

[question:] Is it okay to do when he's not on duty?

My friend and seminary president, Gordon Wetmore, told me about a couple of signs he saw.

Both were scrawled in large, conspicuous letters on an old general store in New England.

The one over the entrance announced:

> **𝔄𝔫𝔱𝔦𝔮𝔲𝔢𝔰 𝔉𝔬𝔯 𝔖𝔞𝔩𝔢**

But around back, he spotted a sign over the exit that read:

> **We buy junk**

Contrasting viewpoints to be sure. One for selling; the other for buying.

A sign (plaque), on the wall of a faculty office at Pepperdine, communicates a point of view that all academic "stuffed shirts" need to be reminded of:

> THE PURPOSE OF EDUCATION:
> TO TAKE A PERSON FROM
> COCKSURE IGNORANCE
> TO THOUGHTFUL UNCERTAINTY

Bumper stickers qualify as signs. Many are clever; all disclose a definite point of view. Here is a sampling of ones I've spotted:

HAPPINESS WON'T BUY MONEY!

STAMP OUT OLD AGE – SMOKE CIGARETTES

SAVE A LOGGER – KILL AN OWL

ESCHEW OBFUSCATION

MY KID BEAT UP YOUR HONOR STUDENT

Signs, in the form of posters, seem to be cropping up everywhere. Here's one with a very straight-forward point of view. It is selling something, and who could possibly reject its "pitch?"

HUGGING

IT'S NOT ONLY NICE, IT'S NEEDED.

IT CAN RELIEVE PAIN OR DEPRESSION, MAKE THE HEALTHY HEALTHIER, THE HAPPY HAPPIER, AND EVEN THE MOST SECURE MORE SO.

IT FEELS GOOD, OVERCOMES FEAR, EASES TENSION.

IT PROVIDES STRETCHING EXERCISE IF YOU'RE SHORT, AND STOOPING EXERCISE IF YOU'RE TALL.

IT DOESN'T UPSET THE ENVIRONMENT, SAVES HEAT, AND REQUIRES NO SPECIAL EQUIPMENT.

IT MAKES HAPPY DAYS HAPPIER, AND IMPOSSIBLE DAYS POSSIBLE![1]

One more poster that, I'd venture to say, expresses a point of view that most of us agree with:

FAMILY

If the family were a *container*, it would be a *nest*, an enduring nest, loosely woven, expansive, and open.

If the family were a *fruit*, it would be an *orange*, a circle of sections, held together but separable — each segment distinct.

If the family were a *boat*, it would be a *canoe* that makes no progress unless everyone paddles.

If the family were a *sport*, it would be *baseball*: a long, slow, nonviolent game that is never over until the last out.

If the family were a *building*, it would be an *old, solid structure* that contains human history, and appeals to those who see the carved moldings under all the plaster (and) the wide plank floors under the linoleum. . . .[2]

---

1. Composed by Muriel Kraeger.

2. Letty Cottin Pogrebin, *Family Politics: Love and Power on an Intimate Frontier* (New York: McGraw-Hill, 1983), pp. 25-26.

Ready to flip over to the next section of my scrapbook? It contains quotations that betray definite points of view — expressed in spontaneously refreshing ways.

Well Spoken

O. Henry admonishes us: "Inject a few raisins of (clever words) into the tasteless dough of existence." The following did, and the result is delicious, "verbal pastry." Have a few big bites!

> *"If it's the 'ultimate,' then why are they doing it again next year?"* (N.F.L.'s Hollywood Henderson, on eve of Super Bowl, after reporter asked, "Isn't this the ultimate experience of your life?")

> *"I realize he'd never have any chance of winning, but I figured that the association would do him good"* (old farmer, after a Kentucky Derby track official denied his request to enter his mule in the big race).

> *"My father would have appreciated those kind words, and my mom would have believed them"* (Lyndon Baines Johnson, defusing an introduction that "spread it on" too thick).

> *"One Christmas, as a child, I received a bright, new hammer. Immediately, it seemed like everything in the house needed hammering"* (adult politician, admitting that his point of view pounds home his positions on every issue).

Cited in Kenneth C. Kammeyer, *Marriage and Family: Foundation for Personal Decisions* (Boston: Allyn and Bacon, Inc., 1987), p. 2.

"All people are experts — only on different sub-jects" (Will Rogers, satirizing about the "authori-ties" of our world).

"Microchips matter more than potato chips" (George Will, extolling computer technology).

"The block of granite which is an obstacle in the pathway of the weak, becomes a stepping-stone in the pathway of the strong" (Thomas Carlyle, imply-ing that circumstances aren't determinative).

"Consider the postage stamp, my son. It secures success through its ability to stick to one thing until it gets there" (Josh Billings' advice to his impulsive son).

Minister Robert Schuller had it right when he declared: "Words can be **bullets** or **bombs**, but our task is to make them **blessings**." How? By having minds and hearts that possess healthy, vibrant points of view!

But, let's turn from words to events. Historical occurrences that reflect points of view that, no doubt, sharply contrast with our own.

Getting Historical

Indeed, history records events and actions that seem alien. More than a tad bizarre. Reason: Again, because of the underlying points of view. Ones that seem light-years away from ours. Chew on these:

> ➤ The U.S. Government sought to replenish the stock of horses of the Shoshone Indians, follow-ing battles in which they incurred great losses. The animals were graciously accepted, then

promptly eaten!³

➤ In 1882, Dr. J.H. Kellogg wrote *Plain Facts*, a 504-page sex manual, asserting: "certain foods, especially coffee, stimulate and excite sex organs." Solution? Kellogg recommended "grains that unstimulate." From this conviction sprang the origin of breakfast cereals composed of corn flakes.⁴

Who's to argue with the Shoshones? Our culinary preference for cows, rather than horses, is no more than a cultural preference — carried on by tradition.

And how about old J.H.? His intentions were noble. Today people distribute condoms; back then, he promoted cereal. Funny thing: Both viewpoints claim to be supported by valid, persuasive reasons.

If you think that's strange, check out the point of view undergirding this list of rules. They were posted by a public school principal in New York City. The year? 1872.

---

3. The Western Shoshone lived in the arid habitat of the American Great Basin, which is now Nevada, western Utah, and eastern Oregon. Until the nineteenth century the Shoshone got their meat from deer and antelope (as well as from small mammals such as rabbits). The resemblance of these animals to horses made them a logical food choice. (cf. James Peoples and Garrick Bailey, *Humanity: An Introduction To Cultural Anthropology*, 3rd edition. Los Angeles: West Publishing Company, 1994, pp. 141-142).

4. *L.A. Times*, November 11, 1992, article entitled "The Secret Sex Lives of Snap, Crackle and Pop."

Be it hereby known by all who instruct pupils within the premises of this school's jurisdiction:

1. Teachers each day will fill lamps, clean chimneys & trim wicks.
2. Each teacher will bring a bucket of water and a scuttle of coal for the day's session.
3. Make your pens carefully. Whittle nibs to the individual taste of the pupil.
4. Men teachers may take one evening each week for courting purposes, or two evenings if they attend church regularly.
5. After ten hours in school, the teacher should spend the remaining time reading the Bible or other good books.
6. Women teachers who marry, or engage in unseemly conduct, will be dismissed.
7. Every teacher should lay aside from each payday a goodly sum of his earnings for his benefit during his declining years so that he will not become a burden on society.
8. Any teacher who smokes, uses liquor in any form, frequents pool halls, or gets shaved in a barber shop, will give good reason to suspect his worth, intentions, integrity and honesty.
9. The teacher who performs his labor without fault for five years will be given an increase of twenty-five cents per week in his pay, provided the Board of Education approves.[5]

Clamped tightly with such oppressive strictures, there was little opportunity for "kicking up any heels!" A clear case of "cruel and unusual punish-

---

5. Document's source is unknown.

ment." I can't help but wonder how today's A.C.L.U. might have responded to their plight back then.

And we're only separated from them by time.

But, in a real sense, chasms of divergent viewpoints separate us today. Let's examine how.

In the Same House, But on Different Floors

At the dawn of the 21st century, there are many ways to "slice the American pie." To name a few:

- social class
- political ideology
- leisure preferences
- ethnicity
- education
- religious beliefs
- residence
- income
- physical attributes

To these, allow me to add just one more: *age* (or *generational*) differences.

As small kids our point of view was connected to three key circuits: immediate need-gratification, successful manipulation of authority figures, and satisfying our curiosities. Concerning the latter, most of us "drove our parents up the wall" posing an endless supply of questions like:

"How do worms yawn?"

"Did they call Robin Hood's mom 'Mother Hood?'"

"If a cow laughed, would milk come out her nose?"

"How would chairs look if our legs bent the other way?"

Well, eventually we grow up. Our innocence and naiveté vanish like noontime fog. We look around, and quickly discover that our viewpoints tend to concur with persons in our age group.

Sociologists differentiate unique points of view among:

> ➤ War Babies (still traumatized by the Great Depression, their primary focus is on financial security);

> Baby Boomers (post-World War II's "monster consumers," who spend like crazy and max-out their credit);

> Baby Busters (insecurely face a mammoth national debt, an uncertain job market, and strong prospects of a decreased standard of living).

Obviously, we've focused on economics — a key reality that is, indeed, paramount in crafting each generation's viewpoint. (To examine other generational contrasts, refer to Appendix C.)

After considering these contrasts within America — in yesteryear as well as today — let's broaden our focus to include sharply contrasting points of view in our world.

Pack Your Mental Suitcases

One anthropologist is on target: "What is true about mankind anywhere is significant for mankind everywhere." After all, we're all Homo Sapiens, facing very similar survival challenges, and well able to mutually contribute to each other's well-being. In short, we're more alike than different, and there are tremendous advantages in fully recognizing that fact.[6]

---

6. Anthropologist John Honigmann (1970) enumerates mankind's universal nonbiological needs. They are:

psychological need	forms it can take
◆ Relatedness	◆ Love, submission, wielding power
◆ Transcendence	◆ Creativity, destructivity
◆ Rootedness	◆ Nationalism, racism, brotherhood
◆ Identity	◆ Hero worship, style imitations

Similarly, anthropologist George Peter Murdock, after a cross-cultural comparison of 565 world cultures, lists characteristics they all have in common. Some of these are: bodily adornment, calendar, dancing, etiquette, folklore, incest taboos,

But, in spite of this, the old adage is true: "One culture's 'meat' is another's 'poison'; one culture's 'language' is another's 'gibberish.'"[7]

To restate an earlier point, our "consciousness of kind" prompts us to be culturally bound and blind. Ethnocentrism runs rampant in its three forms: stereotyping (mentally categorizing), prejudice (emotionally rejecting) and discrimination (behaviorally oppressing). And, by falling into this trap, how much we cheat ourselves!

But, the fact remains, we manifest very different viewpoints.

There are broad categories of differences. For example, people in Third World/tribal peoples differ, consistently, from those of us who are First World/modern. (See Appendix D for major differences for a wide assortment of areas.)

Also, there are more specific contrasts. My anthropological studies, and world travels, have provided me with a plethora of examples. I've included them in this, the final section of my scrapbook.

FOOD: To the American palate, the kidney, in England's kidney pie, tastes a lot like burnt inner-tube! Germans have a real thing against eating corn

---

joking, luck superstitions, law, mythology, soul concepts, weather control. (Cf. George Peter Murdock, "The Common Denominator in Cultures," *The Science Of Man In The World Crisis,* ed. Ralph Linton. New York: Columbia University Press, 1945, pp. 123-125.)

7. The English word for "barbaric" originates from the Greek term, *barbarizō.* A loose translation connotes that all foreigners sound, to the Greek ear, like they are mumbling a very unintelligible and offensive-sounding "bar-bar-bar." (from "The Prejudice Film," produced by Max Miller, Narrated by David Hartman, Motivational Media, Los Angeles, CA.)

("the food of schwein"). As for southern China, there's a popular saying: "We eat everything that has four legs — except for tables and chairs." And, believe me, they do. One Canton restaurant advertises that they serve nothing but rat dishes — two dozen or so. I'll spare details about monkeys, scorpions, snakes, cats and puppies.

PROHIBITIONS: Australian Aborigines are prohibited from looking at their mother-in-law. To be seen doing so, is to have one eye burned out. Spitting is thought to be a major offense in Ireland. (They'd go crazy watching players at one of our major league baseball games!) Persons caught with drugs in Malaysia, whether citizens or visitors, are shot.

MORALS: Botocudo (African tribe) women wear ear, lip and nose plugs — bamboo sticks shoved into their skin, causing it to stretch. However, they wear little (if any) clothes. To be "plugless," to them, is to be "immoral." But, to be nude, is to be "normal." By contrast, the Innes Baeg, who reside on an island off the Northern Irish Coast, refuse to learn to boat. Reason: While at sea, a storm might arise, and they just might be tempted to remove their clothes and dive in. Revealing any skin, even during an emergency, is absolutely forbidden.

RITUALS: The Jerusalem Hilton has a "Sabbath Elevator," which, (on Saturdays) works automatically. To push elevator buttons is considered "work," which is forbidden by the Torah. When married, Burmese brides have their cervical vertebrae (necks) stretched, so that many copper rings can go around them. In this extended state, their neck cartilage becomes very weak. If, during their wedded lives, they are discovered cheating on their husbands, the latter need only remove the copper rings. Immediately, the neck will snap and death occurs.

Again, in spite of these extreme differences, we must be admonished to respect others' points of view. It is so basic. So right.

People of all cultures thoroughly absorb the dominant point of view of their milieu. Regardless of how weird it seems to us, it seems perfectly logical (and right) to them. So much so that they'll defend it to the hilt, at the slightest hint of a challenge.

The same is true for cultures and subcultures we encounter in our own land!

In regard to *all* diverse people, it is imperative that we seek to see as others see. To expose ourselves to others' viewpoints — through travel, reading and conversation. After doing this, we'll discover that the three "demons" (stereotypes, prejudices, and discrimination) will start to suffocate. In addition, our point of view will greatly enlarge.

Undeniably, it's a "win-win" situation for everyone!

The "ripple-effect" is felt by others. And they are quite likely to reciprocate. To respond to acceptance by accepting.

Also, we can expect a "boomerang effect." The ripples we send out, eventually, return to impact us. What goes around comes around. What we reap we sow. The impactor is impacted. The respect we show for others is likely to be returned.

We close our scrapbook, having explored numerous, varied points of view. We've focused on persons who frame reality's picture with a very wide assortment of materials, in all sorts of sizes, and for multitudes of contrasting purposes.

My purpose was to dignify, and reveal the beauty of, different viewpoints. To appeal for tolerance and understanding.

But, having said this, I have a definite bias. There is one point of view that stands "head and shoulders" above all the rest. And the whole world can better itself by learning, and accepting, it.

And the Winner Is. . .

Let's reiterate three key facts:

1. We have greater potential for molding our point of view than either experiencing a personal revelation or perfecting our perception.

2. The point of view we mentally sculpt can add marvelous significance, and great comfort, to our lives — especially when we're stuck. In short, it is our best gateway for enlarging, and bettering, our perspective.

3. We can "go to school on" others' points of view. Thus, we are wise to keep a selective, mental scrapbook of the best we encounter. Some to compare, others to contrast, ourselves with.

But, we have yet to answer the most crucial question of all: Is there one, quintessential point of view for all of us — at all times, in all places? One that's absolutely guaranteed to help us relate with the "bozos" who seek to make our lives miserable? Absolutely, 100% yes!

What is it? Put simply, it's the Christian point of view. The one that is exemplified in the life and teachings of Jesus, and emphatically spelled out in the pages of our Holy Bible.

This supreme viewpoint bears looking into. And not just a courteous, cursory glance. Rather, a thorough, open-minded inspection. Our goals? To boil it down to its essence. To discover its incredible value. To apply it to our lives — as we are, right now.

It is time to prayerfully consider the authentic Christian point of view. Piercing through encrustations of tradition, faulty facsimiles, and even personal biases, let's "go for the gold!"

But, just before responding to this great challenge, let's take a quick breather. Looking back, let's grapple with these questions.

1. Which scrapbook item spoke to my mind, or heart, the most? Why? What is its underlying point of view?

2. As I read entries in the author's scrapbook, the following of my own came to mind.

3. Before reading this book's spin on "the Christian point of view," I will state what I think it is as follows:

CHAPTER TEN

A Frame That's Divinely Illuminated

"Our Lord never patches up our natural virtues,
he remakes the whole man on the inside."
(Oswald Chambers)

"The great debate of history:
'To see is to believe.' (Aristotle) 'To believe is to see.' (Paul)"
(Joel Solliday)

"I want to know God's thoughts — the rest are details."
(Albert Einstein)

Prisoners participating in World War II's "Bataan Death March" valued the Bibles they were given. Not because they provided words of courage and comfort for desperate times. Rather, because the thin paper on which they were printed could be easily used for rolling cigarettes.

They valued smoke in their lungs more than truth in their hearts.[1]

By contrast, those of us who are twice-born consider God's Word to be our strength, sustenance, and survival kit. Why? Because its inspired, reliable truths provide an enlightened, authentically

---

1. *Herald of Holiness*, June, 1992, by W.E. McCumber, article entitled "Perspective," p. 44 (Section: "Observer at Large").

Christian point of view — enabling us to see clearly and rightly.

But, more than our mind is impacted. A real number is done on our heart. Allow me to explain.

Coronary Transplant

In a biblical sense, our heart is much more than a blood pump. It is the "seat of our affections." In light of our discussion, it's the "frame shop" of our dominant point of view. Popular devotional writer, Anthony De Mello, sheds this valuable light:

> (We) mistakenly assume that thinking is done by (our) head; it is done actually by the heart which first dictates the conclusion, then commands the head to provide the reasoning (to) defend it.[2]

Proverbs says: "In his heart a man plans his course" (16:9). If our heart focuses on Jesus, internalizes biblical truth, and relies on the Holy Spirit for empowerment and guidance, we'll be "thumbs-up" kind of people. Our outlook will be upbeat and hopeful. Proverbs says:

> *"A happy heart makes the face cheerful"* (15:13);
>
> *". . . the cheerful heart has a continual feast"* (15:15).

By the same token, if our heart spews forth a lot of corruption we'll have tons of grief. The telltale evidence? Our selection of words. Jesus declares:

> *". . . the things that come out of the mouth come from the heart, and these make a man unclean.*

---

2. Anthony De Mello, *The Way to Love: The Last Meditations of Anthony De Mello* (New York: Doubleday, 1991), front and back covers.

For out of the heart (can) come evil thoughts, murder, adultery, sexual immorality, theft, false testimony, slander" (Matt. 15:18-19).

As strange as it may seem, our desperate need is for a heart with "enlightened eyes."

According to David Davenport, President of Pepperdine University, we're all gifted with three sets of eyes: those of the body, mind and heart. But, not until the eyes of our heart become illuminated, and we truly see life as God does, do we become "whole" people.[3]

His insight closely parallels Saint Paul's prayer for the Ephesians:

"I pray . . . that the eyes of (their) heart(s) (may be) enlightened (so they) may know the **hope** *to which (they) are called, the* **riches** *of his glorious inheritance in the saints, and his incomparably great* **power** *for us who believe* (Eph. 1:18-19a, emphasis added).[4]

-----

3. David Davenport, *1995 Volunteer Center Yearbook*, front cover.

4. Paul wrote to the Ephesians from a Roman prison. He feared that their spiritual eyes were shut or blinded.

Concerning the *"inheritance,"* one commentator suggests that it is the possession of God Himself. As we give ourselves to Him, He gives Himself to us, the saints.

Ponder these: Do we expect to receive divine discernment in sorting out personal priorities? In finding consensus in the tension of divided opinions in a church board or faculty meeting? In confronting hidden attitudes of those we counsel, or even within ourselves? In formulating career decisions we make? Can we expect God's great power to be at our disposal as we try to be truly Christian in a culture bent on swallowing up Christian values? Can we really expect the Holy Spirit to open our minds, when we read God's Word, to discern truth for today — individually or collectively?

Hope. Inheritance riches. Power. The not-so-shabby derivatives of our enlightenment.

Key point: Our heart's eyes become enlightened when we surrender our lives to Jesus. Why? Because He completely transforms our heart (see Romans 12:1-2). Result: We are given a truly Christian point of view. One that's certain to bring total newness of mind, heart and sight. (cf. 2 Cor. 5:17)

This book is about enlightened vision, which is generated from a purified heart.

It's story time.

Tinsel Torture

Christmas season is an ideal time to observe the vicious tug-of-war between Christian and secular points of view.

During this holiday season, even the most devout of us are well-advised to be especially vigilant — lest we be swept into the materialistic mainstream. But, with enlightened eyes, we can count on God helping us to construct the best possible frame around the entire Season.

The Yuletide Season had arrived. It was time to trim the tree.

Dad and mom began sifting through the boxes of ornaments, as they prepared to decorate. They were used to it by now — tree-trimming and celebrating Christmas alone, that is — for their only son had long since moved across the country.

Well, the project went quite well. Lights were balanced and tested. Next came the bulbs. That's when it happened. Dad glanced down into one of the bulb boxes, and there it was — a bulb with tiny fingerprints. A devastating reminder of the past.

A rush of grief rushed into the lonely father's being. He began to sob.

Mom heard it, looked over, and saw the bulb that he clutched so closely. She instantly understood. Wanting to offer consolation, she struggled for words. But, they would not come. Then tears began to fill her own eyes.

There was more than a tad of self-pity and resentment in both of their hearts. They desperately needed a new perspective, or to be reminded of an old one.

Then like a flash, the "eyes" of mom's heart became enlightened with spiritual insight. The defeating, ugly frame was instantly discarded; one that brought great comfort took its place.

Same condition — no son in sight. But, a new point of view.

Mom, in a soft voice, shared these simple words with her troubled husband: "My dear, a Father saying 'good-bye' to His Son is, in reality, what Christmas is all about."

Dad smiled. A light of inspiration flickered, then shone brightly. He tightly squeezed mom's hand as they shared a prayer. The tree-trimming resumed.[5]

"Fingerprinted Christmas Bulbs" — Our Destiny

Sure, a story is a story is a story. It's purely anecdotal. Relevant to only the people involved at one point in time. But is it really? Perhaps, within it there is significance for all of us.

We all have our story, with a criss-cross of plots, people and places.

---

5. Excerpted from a Christmas message, 1991, by Norman Shoemaker.

Things happen. Our emotions bounce around — from pure ecstasy to excruciating pain.

Often there is little we can do to alter our circumstances. I'm reminded of something my mother, a registered nurse, used to say: "Life is like medicine labels, the directions say 'take it.'"

What matters most when one of life's "fingerprinted Christmas bulbs" pops up to activate painful memories? Or regrets? Or self-pity? It's at that very moment that we must be open to the perspective that God has for us.

It can come quicker than airmail special delivery! Sometimes it is slower. Also, the form it takes can vary: a new biblical slant; an insightful comment of a caring friend; an inspiring thought. But, whenever or however it arrives, its value is immense!

The result? In a word, relief. So that we're able to cope — not just somehow, but triumphantly!

Recall my church story. It was a painful chapter in my life. Even more so, it was frustrating.

> ➤ I tried everything I knew to *change* things: others, circumstances, myself. Results? Nada. Zilch. *Strike One.*

> ➤ Frustrated, I hoped for mere *communication.* At least, all parties could dialog. And we did — for awhile. But, before long, my protagonists turned their backs, ignored my good-faith overtures, and let it be known that they were "finished talking" — except behind my back. *Strike Two.*

> ➤ Dejected, I stumbled back to my final option. My goal became simply to *cope.* To just keep on keeping on, not expecting nor demanding improvement. But, still, never blaming the Lord.

Is coping possible under such circumstances? When there's not even a speck of light at the end of the tunnel? Without a doubt.

I found that, at my time of greatest desperation, my heart became completely open to His point of view. And He didn't let me down.

He gave me a new grip; new and clear sight; renewed purpose for living. But best of all, my well-being was no longer dependent on circumstances changing — nor even effective communication.

My frustration subsided. A deep and abiding peace returned.

In spite of the fact that there has been no "fairy-tale ending."

I'm reminded of General William Booth, founder of the Salvation Army, on his deathbed. When asked how things were going he replied: "The waters are rising." Then, with diminishing breath he added: "But, praise be to God, I am rising with the waters."

No miraculous reversal in his health condition. His heavenly Father simply gifted him with a heavenly point of view. One that made his transition to the next life triumphant!

Similarly, my situation is far more tolerable. I maintain perpetual hope that true reconciliation can someday occur. But if not, it's okay. The pain has subsided. Unconditional forgiveness has been extended. And, as a huge bonus, I have deepened in my walk with our Lord.

What triggered the change in my point of view?

No visions nor miracles. No faxes from heaven. No motivational seminars. Nothing spectacular enough to report on the Christian Broadcasting Network!

The "aha event" occurred while listening to our

friend and pastor, Steve Green, speak on a typical Sunday morning. In graphic, inspiring words, he presented the essence of a Christian perspective. He spelled out how I could get unstuck!

Revisiting God's Word For the "First Time"

Who among us hasn't had familiar Scripture come alive? Suddenly, we begin to unpack new, inspiring, practical insights. It's like we understand words we've always heard, for the very first time!

God does a beautiful job of recycling His rich, multi-dimensional, biblical truths in our hearts. So that our point of view is more in alignment with His. I say this from firsthand experience.

Back to that red-letter Sunday morning. Steve chose Mark, chapter 4, as his text. He focused on Christ's well-known Parable of the Sower. In particular, he spotlighted the second kind of soil. The type located in "rocky places," and described as "shallow" (v. 5).

He set the stage: in Israel, then as today, much of the land appears suitable for growing crops. Seeds planted do, in fact, flourish. But then, after their tender roots hit the hardscrabble layer (3"-5" deep), they wither. Soon the sun scorches them, and they die (v. 6).

Was this parable a Biology 101 lecture, to enlighten our Lord's educationally-impoverished followers? Hardly — Jesus had a deep, pertinent, spiritual message in mind. And it was directed, squarely, at His disciples.

He recalled how they had *"sprung up quick"* — enthusiastically dropping their nets to follow Him (1:18, 20). Again, theirs was a fast, decisive beginning.

But now, He could see their downward trajectory.

They were banging their roots against a hard layer of rock. Prognosis? They were far from being stay-with-the-stuff kind of fellows. Rather, it was plain to see that they were wishy-washy. Mickey Mouse. Shallow. True flakes.

Result? They were stuck. They didn't understand the "big picture," and they'd never get with the program until they did!

Let's pinpoint the times their shallowness was exposed:

➤ No comprehension of His Parable of the Sower.
(Jesus) *"Don't you understand this parable? How then will you understand any parable?"* (4:13).

➤ Shortsightedness prior to Jesus feeding the 5,000.
(Disciples) *"Send the people away so they can go . . . and buy something to eat."* Then, after Jesus told them that they would be supplying the food, they replied: *"That would take eight months wages!"* (6:36-37).

➤ Lack of understanding, just after Jesus had walked on the Sea of Galilee to rescue them from a storm.
(Mark's description) *"They were completely amazed . . . their hearts were hardened"* (6:51-52)

➤ Doubt and frustration just before Jesus fed the 4,000.
(Disciples) *"Where in this remote place can anyone get enough bread to feed them?"* (8:4).

➤ Worry because they had forgotten to bring bread.
(Jesus) *"Why are you talking about having no bread? Do you still not see or understand? Are*

*your hearts hardened? Do you have eyes but fail
to see . . . ?"* (8:17-18).

(Jesus asked them to recall the two bread miracles, and how much surplus food was gathered
after all were full.)

➤ Rebuke of Jesus (by Peter), after He said that
He must die and be resurrected.

(Jesus) *"You do not have in mind the things of
God, but the things of men. . . . If anyone would
come after me, he must deny himself and take
up his cross and follow me"* (8:33-34).

➤ Unwillingness to understand (accept) Jesus,
when He repeated that He must die and be resurrected.

(Mark's account) *"But they did not understand
what He meant and were afraid to ask him
about it"* (9:32).

➤ Argument concerning "who was greatest."

(Jesus) *"If anyone wants to be first, he must be
the very last, and the servant of all"* (9:35).

After this "Bible-surfing," we ask ourselves: How
did the disciples blow it? What was the consistent
thread that made them underachievers?

A Kingdom Unlike Any Other

The closest followers of our Lord were stuck
because they misunderstood the Kingdom of God.
They tripped up on its two primary cornerstones.
Let's carefully examine each of them.

**First, everything that happens in the King-
dom of God is to be received as a gift — not
something we do, tweak or manipulate.**

Referring to Christ's feeding of both multitudes,
Steve said: "The disciples discovered that there's no

such thing as a 'bread recipe' in God's Kingdom." No special technique nor secret formula — nothing but sheer miracle.

We hear that we need only get fired up, attend some "get-smart" seminar, or commit to try harder. Such efforts will impress God, and He'll treat us especially good.

Not so. The Kingdom of God is wrapped up in one word, "**grace**."[6] Some define it as "unmerited favor." My spiritual father, Earl Lee, thinks of it as "the outgoing energy of the redemptive personality of God washing against the shores of human need."

When I think of it, a bunch of "alls" come to mind. Grace is *all* of God's outrageously extravagant activity, toward *all* of us, throughout *all* of our lives.

Writer Harold Ivan Smith captures this all-inclusiveness: "God distributes grace like a five-year-old spreading peanut butter."

Once again, grace follows us all the days of our lives.

---

6. Lewis Smedes, in *How Can It Be All Right When Everything Is All Wrong?*, asks, "Why do we call grace *amazing*?" His response: "Grace is *amazing* because it works against the grain of common sense."

Hard-nosed *common sense* will tell you that you are too wrong to meet the standards of a holy God; pardoning *grace* tells you that it's all right in spite of so much in you that is wrong.

Realistic *common sense* tells you that you are too weak, too harassed, too human to change for the better; *grace* gives you power to send you on the way to being a better person.

Plain *common sense* may tell you that you are caught in a rut of fate or futility; *grace* promises that you can trust God to have a better tomorrow for you than the day you have made for yourself. (*Christianity Today*, November 13, 1995, in "Reflections: Classic and Contemporary Excerpts," p. 69.)

➤ For starters, by grace we are *given salvation.* Listen to Eugene Petersen's translation of Ephesians 2:8-9:
"Saving is all his idea, and all his work. All we do is trust him enough to let him do it. It's God's gift from start to finish! If we did, we'd probably go around bragging that we'd done the whole thing!"[7]

➤ By grace, God reveals His moral code to those already graced. The law is given a new spin: Rather than being the way we become God's people (legalism), it's how we're enabled to live as faithful people of God.

➤ Through Jesus, who bequeathed us the Holy Spirit, we are given grace that empowers, resources and energizes us to do God's will. Again, hear Petersen's vivid paraphrase:
"Be energetic in your life of salvation, reverent and sensitive before God. That energy is God's energy. . .deep within you, God himself willing and working at what will give him the most pleasure" (Phil. 2:13).[8]

The incredible gift of grace isn't always understood correctly.

At times, we've equated it with cheap sentimentality — God "winking" at (excusing) our evil. But He emphatically commands: *"Consecrate yourselves and be holy, because . . . I am the Lord, who makes you holy"* (Lev. 20:7). Through His grace, we can live holy lives!

Other times we've taken grace for granted — as

---

7. Eugene H. Petersen, *The Message* (Colorado Springs: NavPress, 1994), p. 477.

8. Ibid., p. 491.

many do sunsets and flowers. We've been flip and cavalier, forgetting that grace cost God plenty. Paraphrasing Dietrich Bonhoeffer: We call it "grace" because it is God's gift; but we know it is "costly" because it cost God everything!

Finally, after receiving this unearned gift, we've often become proud and self-righteous. Considering ourselves spiritually elite. Karl Barth hits the bull's-eye in declaring: "Our ultimate ethical response to God, for His grace, must be a life of gratitude." A life lived in continuous, humble worship and obedience. Not something to gloat over.

Lesson #1: It's all based on God's gift of grace. Period. Exclamation point. What is the second crucial principle?

Second, the economy of the Kingdom of God is upside down.

For the true Christian, it's a complete switcheroo in priorities. Power is perfected in weakness; greatness lies in smallness; leadership comes from "the least of these."[9]

It's all about becoming "towel-and-basin" servants (John 13:4). To His disciples He said: *"If anyone wants to be first (in God's Kingdom), he must be the very last, and the servant of all"* (Mark 9:35).

In spite of what we hear in the vicinity of most churches, it's not about who's greatest, smartest, richest. Not the most powerful, most charismatic, or even the most loved. No way.

---

9. French sociologist Emile Durkheim (*The Elementary Forms of Religion*) referred to this principle as the "transvaluation of value." It means: turning the societal value system "on its head," so that whatever is deemed good/right "out there" is considered evil/wrong "in here" — and visa versa.

The most common biblical word for "servant" is *doulos,* meaning "slave." In ancient times, it was a title of great humiliation.

What, specifically, is involved in being a servant of our heavenly Father? William Barclay says it is being:

➤ inalienably possessed by God;

➤ unqualifiedly at the disposal of God;

➤ unquestionably obedient to God;

➤ constantly in the service of God.[10]

And we have the supreme Example to follow: Jesus. The One who declared: *"But I am among you as one who serves"* (Luke 22:27).

Someone said: We can never fill His shoes, but we can walk in His steps. The steps of a servant. And where did His steps eventually lead? Straight to the cross.

Now it's our turn. In His words: *"A student is not above his teacher, nor a servant above his master"* (Matt. 10:24). Forget about any comfort zones or safety privileges. He pulls no punches in telling His disciples: *"If anyone would come after me, he must deny himself and take up his cross and follow me"* (Mark 8:34).

---

10. William Barclay, *The Daily Study Bible: The Letters of James And Peter* (Philadelphia: Westminster, 1955), pp. 345-346.

According to this same commentator, 1 Cor. 4:1 employs the word *huperetēs* for "servant." The term originally meant "a rower on the lower banks of a trireme, one of the slaves who pulled at the great sweeps which moved the triremes through the sea." It was pointed out that some commentators use this as a picture of Christ the pilot, who directs the course of the ship, and Paul as the servant accepting the orders of his Pilot, laboring only as his Master directs. (*Letters To The Corinthians,* p. 40.)

More than anything, the cross story instructed, and motivated, the early church.[11] They accepted that the cross Jesus carried was the one that they must bear. With Paul, they declared: *"I have been crucified with Christ and I no longer live, but Christ lives in me"* (Gal. 2:20).

But, for them, this was a joyful privilege — not a

---

11. According to theologian George A. Lindbeck, there are three ways to "do theology" (i.e., interpret the Bible).

1. Propositional truth: Goes to text, symbol, or tradition and extracts great propositions. Finds a correlation between the propositions and the world. *Problems:* To do this, you need a meta-narrative (i.e., abstractions apart from Scripture). Also, it judges history, archaeology, etc. on equal footing with the Written Word (i.e., the Bible is validated if it finds support elsewhere).

2. Experiential or expressive truth: Views a universal common denominator in all experience. Goal: get below the particulars of any religion, and discover its universal commonalties. The idea is that Christians can learn from all sorts of experiences that they have in common with Buddhists, etc. *Problem:* Total subjectivity. The particularity of Christianity is lost.

3. Cultural linguistic: Believes that the Christian community must embody, and be shaped by, the biblical story. Out of this comes convictions, values, cosmology (view of universe) and identity. More than simple storytelling, it views self within the Kingdom of God narrative (plot line) — and from that comes its view of reality. Indeed, there are truth principles contained in the story, (internal, logical consistency; community "truthing;" and applicability to today's world). But, there is much more involved than our reading the story — as we read it, it "reads our lives and society" as its text. Furthermore, it "calls us to translation and transformation."

The cultural linguistic approach has several advantages. Through the story, we see the plot and character development revealed in Scripture. We, then, apply it to ourselves. Result: We're a part of the story. [Note: In Old Testament times, the morbid duty. Why? Because it provided opportunity for identifying with the suffering of their Lord. Catch the upbeat lilt in Peter's words:

> *"Dear friends, do not be surprised at the painful trial you are suffering . . . rejoice that you partici-pate in the sufferings of Christ . . . if you suffer as a Christian. . .praise God that you bear that name"* (1 Pet. 4:12-13,16).

Furthermore, crossbearing is closely tied into the gift of grace. According to our pastor that Sunday morning, "Grace isn't merely a 'ticket into' (God's Kingdom), it's a 'signup to' (become a servant)!" Put simply, God graces us, to enable us to fulfill His Son's expectation — namely, that we'll become true servants.

How do we get off track, when it comes to the essential, pivotal doctrine of servanthood?

Exodus story was the dominant narrative whereby Jews defined reality — and their place within it. Prior to the second century, early Christians defined themselves within the *Cross story*. Then, during the second century, Apologists (defenders of the faith) began using Greek (Platonic) thought as their mainframe. Their goal: Make Christianity understandable via the Greek worldview. They began translating stories into systemic, propositional truths — and ceased letting the story shape the worldview.

Steve Green advocates getting back to the story.

We need to make present-day reality understandable through the Christian story (termed "reversal inversion"). This has especially promising potential for our postmodern world — a world that seems resistant to meta-narratives; a world with striking parallels with the first two centuries. It worked well then; it will now! (Based on interview with Steve Green, 1995, Pasadena, CA; cf. George A. Lindbeck, *The Nature of Doctrine: Religion And Theology in a Post Liberal Age*, first edition. Philadelphia: Westminster Press, 1984.)

1. At times, we *consider our servanthood a "ladder to His favor."* That's backwards. Instead of "if servant-then-grace," it's "grace-empowering-to-be-servants." To be full-fledged partners with Him in redeeming His world.
2. Other times, we *see servanthood as burden or obligation.* A "slow burn." Misery. Drudgery. But Jesus declares: "*. . . my yoke is easy and my burden is light*" (Matt. 11:30). When is this so? When our "burden of heart" consists of an eagerness to participate with God in convincing His world to accept His grace.

Okay. It's time to recap a bit. We've explored two critically important principles. Principles upon which the entire Kingdom of God is built. Let's summarize:

Doctrine	Symbol	What we do	How our heart should respond	How we get off track
grace	*gift*	*receive*	*gratitude* (in worship)	*sentimentality* *law negated* *pride*
servant-hood	*cross*	*serve*	*privileged* (identify with Christ)	*earn God's favor* *burden or obligation*

Unlearned Lessons

Like so many of us, Christ's disciples had quick-sprouting roots that failed to grow deep. They hit the "rocky ground" of dull understanding and hardheartedness. Result: shortsightedness, halfheartedness, fearfulness. Worst of all: unteachability.

The two crucial lessons of God's Kingdom remained unlearned. Unappreciated. Unapplied.

First lesson: For them, God's grace wasn't at all like a five-year-old spreading peanut butter; more like a Campbell employee sprinkling chicken in soup! Very sparing. Very selective.

With such an attitude, no wonder the pressing, needy masses seemed intrusive — and, doubtlessly, insignificant on God's "chain of command."

Second lesson: Servanthood seemed futile, unnecessary and rather foolish. They jockeyed for position among themselves, and tuned out Christ's words on "crossbearing" — both His and theirs![12]

This story has a happy ending. After Jesus died, and the Holy Spirit came, these same disciples began to recall and apply these essential truths. And it changed everything.

Their point of view became *His* point of view. Result? They saw the world, and their appointed task, with different eyes. The "unbearable" became bearable — in spite of intensified persecution; the "impossible" became possible — in spite of opposing forces of incredible might.

Rather like a timed-release cold pill, our Lord's two central messages "kept going off inside them." Within their minds, as they recollected what He said. Within their hearts, as they were filled with His Spirit.

And we all know what occurred. The entire world was turned "rightside up"; and individuals were turned "rightside in."

The two cardinal principles that the disciples internalized and applied were the identical ones that gripped my heart.

---

12. Entire section, related to the Parable of the Seeds (Soils), extracted from sermon and interview with Steve Green, 1995, Pasadena, CA.

New Light That I Began to See By

As I listened to Steve Green preach that morning, and followed this up with a two-hour conference, my heart welled up within me. Like the disciples, my roots needed to get past stony ground. A hard-shale layer of hurt, self-pity, confusion, doubt. In short, I was stuck.

More than anything, I wanted a truly authentic, 100% Christian point of view. And here it was, plain and simple. Two principles that boil down the gospel to its essence. Principles that got the disciples unstuck; and ones that, without a doubt, could free me too.

After taking a long, deep look at God's grace, I realized that His gift authenticated my existence and confirmed my worth — regardless of others' viewpoints. Furthermore, I became confident that His grace would reach out to those who had sought my demise.

One more thing: God's grace, I knew, would enable and empower me to frame "that experience" in a positive light — reconciliation or no reconciliation. And with that confidence, I joyfully relinquished the future into His hands!

What about servanthood? I realized that I had not handled adversity in a Christian manner. There was chafing, even a desire to somehow recoup what, I felt, was lost. I hadn't learned lessons of willing denial and joyful crossbearing. Why? Because I had not placed the entire scenario on the backdrop of "identifying with Christ's suffering."

In a nutshell, God impacted me with His grace. My eyes gradually became more enlightened. What seemed intolerable — in actuality as well as in memory — became acceptable. And I am eternally grateful to God.

It is my prayer that my experience will help any of us who have hit rocky ground. No calamity. No need to panic. All that's needed are roots that are capable of going deeper — penetrating through hard circumstances and incredible odds.

Surpluses of Dividends!

Section One focused on "Getting Stuck." Section Two beamed its spotlight on "Gaining Sight," the only reliable antidote for relationship impasses.

Now it is time to zero in on the overflow of blessings that accompanies our new, biblical frame of reference. Without a doubt, we can expect to transcend immediate crises. But, beyond that there are serendipitous dividends. Surprise blessings. Unforeseen windfalls. There is a kind of synergistic flow of positive energy that "ripples" throughout our entire being and universe.

Let's unfold the final section, entitled "Getting Strong."

But, before doing so, pause with me to reflect on our discussion in this chapter. Take a little time to give these questions your "best shot."

1. How would I describe the "seeing" quality of my mind? Of my heart? In particular, how do I "see" when bogged down in relationship impasses?

2. What "fingerprinted Christmas bulbs" have popped up in my life? How did I react? Why in this way? How could I have responded in a more Christian manner?

3. What are my thoughts about grace? About servanthood? Has this chapter enlarged my vision concerning these crucial truths?

Growing Strong

CHAPTER ELEVEN

Unanticipated Consequences

*"We must always change, renew, rejuvenate ourselves,
otherwise we harden."*
(Goethe)
"The key to immortality is living a life worth remembering."
(Saint Augustine)
"We can't all be shining stars, but we can all twinkle a little."
(Source Unknown)

Possessing an optimistic, wisely-framed perspective is like taking a refreshing "dip" in a pool, breathing mountain air, listening to romantic music, raising the window shade to let sunshine in.

Having a Christian perspective is all of these and more. It's like starting life anew — so that it's transformed, rejuvenated, and infused with spiritual meaning. Hope abounds.

Sure, we who share this viewpoint will still get stuck. Some might even consider themselves appointed by God to give us grief. But, ours won't be an existence of desperation — like the fellow who snarled: "Life's no more than a sexually-transmitted disease with a terminal prognosis."

We'll see the light. We'll keep the faith. With the Holy Spirit's counsel, we'll give our circumstances the best possible spin. We'll deliberately construct a "frame" that's a masterpiece.

And if we'll just hold steady, trust, and obey, a lot of positive things are certain to occur. All of these will serve to make us stronger: more resilient; less prone to self-pity and counterproductive behavior patterns. We'll train our minds to focus on the "twin peaks" of Christian living: a deep, continuous gratitude for God's grace; and, an unswerving commitment to crossbearing servanthood. And, again, His Spirit will help us to see how these have crucial repercussions for all of life.

Our initial motivation may have been limited to the short-range goal of getting unstuck. Of rising above a tormenting relationship that seems to be intensifying and deteriorating by the second. But by buying into a truly Christian point of view, we're not only set free — we're geared-up to begin living.

In short, God goes overboard in His generosity. He fills the cup to the brim but then, as the Psalmist declares, makes it spill over (Ps. 23:5). He delights in giving us serendipitous bonuses. Unexpected dividends. Surplus blessings.

In Section Three, we will explore four of these. They have to do with:

1. facing up to life's **"wilderness experiences,"** courageously and effectively
2. maximizing relationships with **others**
3. seeing **ourselves** — actually and potentially — in the best possible manner
4. relating to **God** as caring Father.

It's time to focus on these satisfying and significant dividends. But, just before launching into this encouraging disclosure, let's call an unofficial "time-out."

166

A Temple, An Altar, A Prayer

After reminding ourselves of God's lavish grace, and the privilege we have of crossbearing, it's appropriate for us to pause and prayerfully reflect. Right here. Right now. No need to travel to a designated *temple* of God. Paul explains that our body, when inhabited by the Holy Spirit, is a temple (1 Cor. 6:19). All it needs is an assenting mind, a loving heart and a willing voice.

Nor do we require a special *altar*. Our present location, no matter where, instantly becomes our altar when dedicated to worship.

So without delay, let's spontaneously respond to our heavenly Father in our own unique way:

➤ *offering* Him gratitude for His magnanimous gift of grace;

➤ *submitting* to Him in humble servanthood, and *committing* to Him to bear His cross;

➤ *asking* Him to help us see everything from His point of view;

➤ *seeking* His forgiveness for times we haven't in the past.

Now, let's take a while to open our minds and hearts to what He has to say to us. About a time when we were stuck. A time when our roots were shallow. A time when our point of view was causing us grief.

About a hope that things will turn around. A trust that we've learned some valuable lessons through trial. A promise that we'll remain true to the viewpoint He has shared in His Word.

Should you wish, feel free to journal below. First, concerning the communication that occurred between you and God. Second, relating to what you are thinking and feeling at the present time.

A Place to Jot Down My Heart's Notations

date: _____   place: _____
time: _____

CHAPTER TWELVE

A Compass for the Wilderness

"Only eyes washed by tears can see clearly."
(Louis L. Mann)
*"God does not give us an over-coming life —
He gives us life as we overcome,"*
(Oswald Chambers)
"Pain is inevitable; misery is optional."
(Source Unknown)

When we accept a new set of eyes, and begin to
see things from a biblical perspective, the results are
astounding! We position ourselves to experience
"abundant life," — the life promised by our Savior
(John 10:10).

In the words of seminary president and author,
David McKenna, clarity of vision prompts us to:

stretch our minds — to discern truth;

search our hearts — to understand our underlying motives;

serve humanity — to become "Christ" to our
world.[1]

---

1. When David McKenna was president at Seattle Pacific
University, Seattle, WA, he offered these three institutional
goals in the school's alumni publication. McKenna went on to
preside over Asbury Theological Seminary, Wilmore, KY, and
author various works.

Who could possibly wish for a life more abundant?

At times, our abundance is a "sleighfull" of immediate earthly blessing. Success — power, privilege, prestige, possessions.[2] Incredible health. Mental tranquility. Perpetually answered prayers. Good luck. Faithful friends. Total comfort. Divine protection.

Unfortunately, some of us so blessed presume that God's children deserve (and are promised) a "rose garden" existence — minus all thorns and aphids!

Deep down, we somehow feel that God will always come through for us. He's our Babe Ruth in life's "bottom of the ninth," our General MacArthur for life's many "wars," our Albert Einstein for making life's most complex problems as simple as "Toys R Us" puzzles.

He's the ultimate Winner, who desires to make each of *us* one!

No grappling with perplexing questions. No struggling with nagging uncertainties. No agonizing with endless suffering. Others may languish in the wilderness, but we only look forward to "cruising along" — and even in style!

Then, with about as much warning as a toddler's temper tantrum, reality rears its grotesque counte-

---

2. Success implies the attainment of cultural goals, and is directly related to one's perceived importance within that culture. In practical terms, its components are:
 ➤ power — having commands obeyed and wishes granted;
 ➤ privilege — being given special rights or favors;
 ➤ prestige — receiving acclaim for rising on the social ladder;
 ➤ possessions — material bounty, with attention to quantity as well as quality.
See Jon Johnston, *Christian Excellence: Alternative to Success* (Grand Rapids: Baker Book House, 1985; reprint Brentwood, TN: J.K.O. Publishers, 1996), pp. 30f.

nance. Suddenly, our trail becomes incredibly steep, and filled with jagged rocks and hidden holes.

The check *didn't* come in the mail. The cancer *didn't* disappear. The boss *didn't* retract his decision to let us go. *Good* days turn to *bad* days; then, bad days become "*dog* days."

And, to our consternation, this all happens while we're walking obediently. While we're sensing God's light — brightly, and warmly, illuminating our way.

But, before indulging in self-pity, we need to focus on the lives of other exemplary, obedient servants of Jesus.

We hear voices from the past. The Apostle Paul bemoans his "thorn in the flesh" (2 Cor. 12:7). Fox's *Book of Martyrs* discloses unimaginable suffering of yesteryear's saints.

Eighteenth-century reformer, theologian, and preacher, John Wesley, once testified: "Fortune" is hardly a passing acquaintance of mine, but I am intimately related to his daughter, "Misfortune."

How about our present day? Consider Billy Graham, who suffers with Parkinson's disease; Mother Teresa, who is plagued by an erratic heart; our good friends, and deeply committed Christians, Rick and Joyce. Their son Michael's complex, debilitating disease continues to worsen, as they continue to remain true to the Lord.

We all know such stories. And some of us play more than "bit parts" in such sad dramas. We are the leading characters. And the "play" seems to never end!

Furthermore, when we experience the harsh wilderness, we're extremely vulnerable to confusion and disillusionment.

Worst of all, we may be tempted to even resent

our loving heavenly Father. We may irreverently ask: "How dare He treat us, His 'favorite children', so cruelly — or, at least, fail to protect us from harm's way?!"

But at such low times, if we dare turn to God's Word, we're assured a corrective for our myopic vision. We can gain a perspective that will not only help us survive, but become exceedingly stronger in responding to future setbacks!

Job doesn't mince words in declaring our universal, inevitable human predicament: *"Yet man is born to trouble as surely as sparks fly upward"* (Job 5:7). Interpretation: there's a real likelihood that we're going to stumble — and skin our knees. It's "par" for "life's obstacle course." And this usually occurs without the slightest warning.[3]

In reality, we're all only a phone call or letter away from the wilderness. We hear of a:

➣ *sibling*, influenced by the "wrong crowd" to be led astray;

➣ *parent*, depressed by a doctor's unfavorable report;

➣ *friend*, demolished by the loss of a job;

➣ *family*, saddened by the sudden death of a loved one.

---

3. "**5:7** *man is born to trouble.* See 14:1; proof that no one is righteous in the eyes of God (see 4:17-19) . . . *sparks.* Lit. 'sons of Resheph.' In Canaanite mythology, Resheph was a god of plague and destruction. 'Sons of Resheph' is used as a poetic image in the OT for fire . . . bolts of lightning (Ps 78:48) and pestilence (Dt 32:24; Hab 3:5)." *The N.I.V. Study Bible: New International Version*, Kenneth Barker, General Editor (Grand Rapids, Zondervan Publishing House, 1985), p. 730.

Welcome to the Inevitable

To put it plain and simple, as earthly beings, we're bound to land — and bounce around — in life's wilderness. And, make no mistake about it, *we know when we're there!*

Recently, a bunch of college students were asked: "How do you know when you're having a 'wilderness experience'?" Their off-the-wall responses were predictable. It's when:

➢ your parents phone you, and ask *you* for money;

➢ McDonald's refuses to serve you;

➢ you can't decide whether you're "in love," or just have the flu.

As a university prof, at times, I've found myself lost among the "sand dunes." My lecture didn't seem to be hitting home — or else, my students were focused on an upcoming ballgame or "hot" date. About the only thing they were attentive to was their watch!

At times, Jesus experienced similar disappointment. He employed parables, object lessons, scriptural teaching, and numerous other methods to get His crucially important message across. But, His audience wasn't always responsive.

I broke into a smile, when I spotted this the other day:

THE LESSON

Then Jesus took his disciples up on the mountain, and gathering them around him, he taught them saying:

> *Blessed are the poor in spirit, for theirs is the kingdom of heaven,*
> *Blessed are the meek,*
> *Blessed are the merciful,*

Blessed are they that thirst for justice,
Blessed are you when persecuted,
Blessed are you when you suffer,
Be glad and rejoice for your reward is great in heaven,

Then Simon Peter said: *Are we supposed to know this?*
And Andrew said, *Do we have to write this down?*
And James said, *Will we have a test on this?*
And Philip said, *I don't have any paper.*
And Bartholomew said, *Do we have to turn this in?*
And John said, *The other disciples didn't have to learn this.*
And Matthew said, *May I go to the boys' room?*
And Judas said, *What does this have to do with real life?*

Then one of the Pharisees asked to see Jesus' lesson plan and inquired of Jesus,

Where is your anticipatory set and your objectives in the cognitive domain?
And Jesus wept.[4]

Of course, this was but one of many wilderness experiences our Lord endured — along with the accompanying frustration and grief. Yet, He didn't panic nor give up.

And that is why He understands our wilderness experiences so completely and compassionately.

Furthermore, He offers us His compass to chart our course out of the wilderness. Or, at least, out of the discouragement that wilderness experiences can cause. His words are like an oasis: *"In this world you*

---

4. Source unknown.

will have trouble. But take heart! I have overcome the world" (John 16:33).

As His disciples, with transformed perspectives, we're well equipped to approach harsh adversity with confidence and direction.

By contrast, it's no secret that persons without the Lord often react to life's "broadsides" and "cave-ins" with cold stoicism, wild panic, irreverent oaths, or outright denial. They completely blitz-out! The waters of life inundate them.

Even more tragic, they fail to perceive any meaning or significance in their suffering — as evidenced in a statement by comedian W.C. Fields when asked: "How do you respond to life's hardships?" His response: "I have mixed emotions — *nausea* and *disgust!*"

But enough talk. It's time to grab our hiking boots, pup tent and canteen. Let's head for the wilderness. Let's feel the scorching desert wind against our cheeks, see the circling buzzards and scampering jackrabbits, touch the prickly cactus fruit and soft sand. Nothing can equal a firsthand wilderness experience!

Now, I'm not proposing that we trek alone. In our mind's eye, let's accompany two very significant, biblical excursions into this desolate environment. Furthermore, let's try to experience a small dose of what these persons experienced — and learn some helpful lessons.

EXCURSION #1: Land of Lizards

event: beginning of the Exodus, immediately after Pharaoh's armies had been drowned in the sea

> **date:**   approximately 1446 B.C.[5]
> **people involved:** Moses, Aaron, nearly three million Israelites *and us* looking on
> **Bible Passage:**   Exodus 15-16

We know the background. The Book of Exodus provides the whole scoop.

The Israelites endured torturous conditions in Egypt. *"The Israelites groaned in their slavery"* (2:23). Exception: the "abandoned child," Moses, who was raised by his mother, under the extravagant sponsor-

---

5. "In historical terms, the exodus from Egypt was ignored by Egyptian scribes and recorders. No definitive monuments mention the event itself, but a stele of Pharaoh Merneptah (c. 1225 B.C.) claims that a people called Israel were encountered by Egyptian troops somewhere in northern Canaan.

"Finding precise geographical and chronological details of the period is problematic, but new information has emerged from vast amounts of fragmentary archaeological and inscriptional evidence. Hittite cuneiform documents parallel the ancient covenant formula governing Israel's 'national contract' with God at Mount Sinai.

"The Late Bronze Age (c. 1550-1200 B.C.) was a time of major social migrations. Egyptian control over the Semites in the eastern Nile delta was harsh, with a system of brickmaking quotas imposed on the labor force, often the landless, low-class 'Apiru.' Numerous Canaanite towns were violently destroyed. New populations, including the 'Sea Peoples,' made their presence felt in Anatolia, Egypt, Palestine, Transjordan, and elsewhere in the eastern Mediterranean.

"Correspondence from Canaanite town rulers to the Egyptian court in the time of Akhenaten (c. 1375 B.C.) reveals a weak structure of alliances, with an intermittent Egyptian military presence and an ominous fear of people called 'Habiru' ('Apiru')." *N.I.V. Study Bible*, p. 106; see also the discussion of chronology on p. 83 of that work.

ship of Pharaoh's daughter (2:1-10).[6]

Upon reaching his young adult years, Moses assumed a wide variety of significant roles:

- *Murderer*: He impulsively killed an Egyptian beating a Hebrew, only to be reprimanded by a kinsman (2:11-14).
- *Fugitive*: He fled Pharaoh's wrath, for committing the crime, and resided in Midian (2:15).
- *Groom*: After saving the seven daughters of Jethro from some obnoxious shepherds, he married one of the daughters, and became father to Gershom (2:16-23).
- *Shepherd*: He tended the flocks of Jethro (3:1).
- *Liberator*: From a burning bush, an angel commissioned him to return to Egypt and free his people. (3:2-4:17). He balked at the plan, but *not nearly as much as Pharaoh* (7:14-12:30)!

We mostly know Moses as "designated liberator" par excellence. Pharaoh had issued his exit visa. The Israelites headed for the border. To add a little drama, God assigned a cloud and angel to accompanied them.

Flaky Pharaoh, then, changed his mind, and ordered his massive, swift armies to retrieve them. Somehow, the rag-tag Jews reached the sea. Their leader reached out his hand, like a magic wand, and the waters rolled back to clear a pathway. God's people crossed safely.

Not "clued in" this was a B.I.O. (by invitation only) excursion, Pharaoh's armies attempted to cross. Up goes Moses' hand again, and bingo, down come the waters.

---

6. Pharaoh's daughter is, perhaps, the famous 18th-dynasty princess who later became Queen Hatshepsut. Ibid., p. 89.

From the Egyptians' perspective, it was tragic. Also, very baffling. But, for the Jews, it was an event to be ever remembered and treasured. A mega-miracle. Even more, a confirmation of God's goodness.

Free at last! No more of Pharaoh's harassment or dirty looks. Moses and Miriam began whipping up a duet of thanksgiving (15:1-21). And they were "stoked!" I hope they sang on key, for their song went on . . . and on.

OK. So the party ended. The cleanup committee took down the crepe paper, picked up the Dixie cups, and disassembled all folding tables. It was time to move on. Onward to the Promised Land!

But first, there was a gigantic "hoop" to jump through. It was the wilderness. Negotiating its rugged terrain made them very unhappy campers. The Bible tells us that as soon as they began trekking in the Desert of Sin, *"the whole community grumbled against Moses and Aaron"* (16:1-2).

Their attitude resembles today's sports fan, who demands of his favorite athlete: "What have you done for me *lately?!*" Forget about past victories. Past glory. Only the present performance counts.

What, specifically, did the people of Israel complain about?

➤ *Food.* Moses went to God. God responded by promising quail and manna (*"tasted like wafers made with honey"* 16:31).

➤ *Water At Rephidim ". . . Moses cried out to the Lord, 'What am I to do . . . they are almost ready to stone me'"* (17:4). God responded by making the rock at Horeb gush forth water.

Most tragically, the grumbling at Moses and Aaron was, in reality, directed toward God. It was a doubting of His efficacy and wisdom. A complete denial of His sovereignty.

This conclusion is verified later, while impatiently awaiting Moses' return from Mt. Sinai. They *"gathered around Aaron and said, 'Come make us gods, who will go before us'"* (32:1).

Aaron turned superwimp, collected their gold, and formed it all into a golden calf (Egyptian god). Then, adding insult to injury, he directed a festival of revelry and idolatry.

Sure, they got theirs all right. A severe reprimand. And, a mouthful of gold dust. Moses ground up their ridiculous idol, poured the smashed residue in water, and forced them to have "golden calf cocktail." (v. 20)

Amazing what happened in that wilderness. Moses "blew his cool" one time too many. God ordered that he be buried on desolate Mt. Nebo, after being given only a bird's-eye view of the Promised Land (34:1-4).

Escape from Pharaoh was sensational. So was escape from Egypt's diseases, enforced bondage and make-believe gods.

But, then came the scorching, trial-plagued wilderness — with its headaches and heartaches. On second thought, I'm glad we weren't there!

But, in our "mind's eye," let's venture to another wilderness — one experienced by Jesus at a crucial time in His ministry.

EXCURSION #2: Satan's Three Strikes

event: temptations of Christ, immediately after He had been baptized by John in the Jordan River

date: approximately A.D. 27, when Jesus was thirty years old, at the start of His public ministry

people involved: Jesus Christ, Satan, *and us* (and wild animals) looking on

Bible Passage: Matthew 4:1-11

The Gospel writers stress the immediacy with which temptations followed the baptism of Jesus. It was like bang-bang (see Mark 1:12; Luke 4:1-13). Similarly, we recall that in excursion #1, wilderness agonies occurred on the heels of Pharaoh's armies' involuntary dunking.

The principle is obvious, and clearly stated by respected British commentator William Barclay: "It is one of the great truths of life that after every great moment there comes a moment of reaction — and . . . it is in the reaction that the danger lies."[7]

Just after our resistance power is the highest, it often plunges to its lowest. We become more vulnerable. Perhaps, less vigilant.

The tempter carefully, subtly, and skillfully chose such a time to attack our Lord. He had just been dra-

---

7. "That is what happened to Elijah. With magnificent courage Elijah in all his loneliness faced and defeated the prophets of Baal on Mt. Carmel (*I Kings 18:17-40*). That was Elijah's greatest moment of courage and of witness. But the slaughter of the prophets of Baal provoked the wicked Jezebel to wrath, and she threatened Elijah's life. 'And when he saw that, he arose and went for his life and came to Beersheba' (*I Kings 19:3*). The man who had stood fearlessly against all comers is now fleeing for his life with terror at his heels." (William Barclay, *The Daily Study Bible: The Gospel of Matthew*, Volume 1, Philadelphia: The Westminster Press, 1958, p. 57.)

matically affirmed in baptism.[8]

> ➤ The humble pronouncement of John: *"I baptize you with water. But one more powerful than I will come, the thongs of whose sandals I am not worthy to untie"* (Luke 3:16).

> ➤ The opening of heaven, and the descent of God's Spirit — in the form of a dove, that plunked right down on Jesus.

> ➤ The booming voice from heaven: *"This is my Son, whom I love; with him I am well pleased"* (Matt. 3:17). The magic words, from Psalm 2:7, accepted by every Jew as the exact description of their Messiah.

But, let's take a plunge into the scenario and see how it all unfolded — focusing on the passage in Matthew 4.

The Spirit (not Satan) led our Lord into the wilder-

---

8. "Never in all history before this had any Jew submitted to being *baptized*. The Jews knew and used baptism, but only for proselytes who came into Judaism from some other faith. It was natural that the sin-stained, polluted proselyte should be baptized, but no Jew had ever conceived that he, a member of the chosen people, a son of Abraham, assured of God's salvation, could ever need baptism. Baptism was for sinners, and no Jew ever conceived of himself as a sinner shut out from God, for was he not . . . safe for eternity? For the first time in their national history the Jews realized their own sin and their own clamant need of God. Never in all history had there been such a unique national movement of penitence and of search for God.

"This was the very moment for which Jesus had been waiting. Men were conscious of their sin and conscious of their need of God as never before. This was His opportunity, and in His baptism He identified Himself with the search of men for God. When Jesus went to be baptized He was identifying Himself with the men He came to save, in the hour of their new consciousness of their own sin, and of their search for God." (Barclay, pp. 52-53, italics added).

ness to be *tempted*. To be tempted? Wasn't He inviting trouble? Who needs such a "bummer" experience?

Our questions reflect an unfortunate, widespread misunderstanding of the phrase "to tempt" (Gr. *peirazein*). We think it to be inseparably connected with enticement to do wrong.

Although this is sometimes implied, here the term conveys a much more positive slant. It means "to test." This is clearly seen in an instance when ". . . *God did tempt Abraham* . . ." (Gen. 22:1 KJV). The time had come for a supreme test (or demonstration) of his loyalty — as was the case with Jesus.[9]

Underscoring this point, Barclay provides this helpful analogy:

> Just as metal has to be tested far beyond any stress and strain that it will ever be called upon to bear, before it can be used for any useful purpose, so a man has to be tested before God can use him for His purposes.[10]

Similarly, the Jews had a saying:

> The Holy One, Blessed be His Name, does not elevate a man to dignity till He has first tried

---

9. "It is unthinkable that God should try to make any man a wrong-doer. It is inconceivable that God should be the agent in seeking to make any man a sinner. . . .

"Now here is a great and uplifting truth. What we call *temptation* is not meant to make us sin; it is meant to enable us to conquer sin. It is not meant to make us bad, it is meant to make us good. It is not meant to weaken us, it is meant to make us emerge stronger and finer and purer from the ordeal. Temptation is not the penalty of being a man, temptation is the glory of being a man. It is the test which comes to a man whom God wishes to use." (Barclay, pp. 55-56, italics added)

10. Ibid.

and searched him; and if he stands in temptation, then He raises him to dignity.[11]

So where, exactly, did this testing take place? In the wilderness, a 35x15 mile area extending between Jerusalem and the Dead Sea. The Old Testament calls it "Jeshimmon," which means "The Devastation" — an on-target description.

I shut my eyes and see it, having visited the mysterious area upon numerous occasions. The ground is strewn with yellow sand, crumbling limestone, and scattered shingle. There are the contorted strata, with warped and twisted ridges running in all directions. Hills resemble dust heaps. Limestone is blistered and peeling. Rocks are bare and jagged.

Often the ground sounds hollow, when tread upon by human feet or horse's hooves. It glows and shimmers with heat, like a gigantic furnace. It gradually descends toward the Dead Sea, a drop of twelve hundred feet. A drop of limestone, flint, and marl — through crags, corries, and precipices — down to the salty water.[12]

Not a place where most of us would want to picnic! That is, unless we're Bedouins or jackrabbits.

The terrain, alone, would be too much for most of us. But, our Lord chose to fast forty days and nights. In boxing language, He "trimmed down to fighting weight!" After this, in the understatement of all times, *"he was hungry"* (Matt. 4:2). Hungry? Try famished out of His senses!

It was at that point that the devil appeared with his "bag of enticing temptations" — ones that could

---

11. Ibid., p. 56.
12. Ibid.

only lure someone with supernatural powers. In a real sense, we're all tempted through our gifts.

> If *beautiful,* we're tempted to be vain and condescending.

> If *super intelligent,* we're enticed to play "mind games" for personal advancement.

> If *rich,* we're pulled toward materialism and greed.

Furthermore, it follows that the most gifted among us experience the greatest intensity of temptation. Nobody knew this more than Jesus, as He entered the "batter's box" to take Satan's three "best pitches" — all vicious "curveballs!"

Temptation #1: (After showing him a desert littered with little round pieces of limestone rock, which appeared like little loaves:) *"If you are the Son of God,* **tell these stones to become bread***"* (Matt. 4:3)

> *Potential appeals:* A. use powers selfishly; B. bribe people to become followers with bread.

> *His response: "It is written: 'Man does not live on bread alone, but on every word that comes from the mouth of God'"* (see Deut. 8:3).

Temptation #2: (After taking Him to the highest point of the Temple — where Solomon's and the Royal porches met, 450 feet above the Kidron Valley — Satan said:) *"If you are the Son of God . . .* **throw yourself down.** *For it is written: 'He will command his angels concerning you, and they will lift you up in their hands, so that you will not strike your foot against a stone'"* (4:5-6, emphasis added)

> *Potential appeal:* enhance prestige by performing a dramatic stunt.

> *His response: "It is also written: 'Do not put the Lord your God to the test'"* (see Deut. 6:16).

Temptation #3: (After accompanying Him to a towering mountain, and displaying all the kingdoms of the world, he said:) *"All this I will give you . . . if you will bow down and worship me"* (4:9, emphasis added).

> *Potential appeal:* advance by retreating — conquer through compromise.

> *His response: "Away from me, Satan! For it is written: 'Worship the Lord your God, and serve him only'"* (see Deut. 6:13).

The devil's three pitches were all strikes. Jesus slammed each into the next zip code! The "pitcher of deception" dejectedly walked off the mound that day. We read: *"Then the devil left him, and angels came and attended him"* (4:11).

Our Lord entered the wilderness, absorbed its punishment, and emerged with a humongous victory "under His belt." A victory that gave Him great joy, confidence, and poise — for the crucial, future battles He was destined to face!

Two epic wilderness encounters saturated with eternal significance. Valuable lessons for those involved — but also for us. Events that offer rich, timely perspective that help us to "frame" our circumstances. So that we see our inevitable date(s) with the wilderness clearly — and rightly.

What are the crucial principles revealed in these wilderness accounts? Let's take the time to carefully decipher them.

God's Place of Formation

A few months ago, at a Forest Home laymans' retreat, Cherry and I were inspired by Norm Shoemaker's insights concerning "lessons *only learned* in the wilderness." He, likewise, referred to the Exodus and temptation accounts.

What he said has relevance for every wilderness we experience — whether it involve disintegrating health, overwhelming depression, loss of employment, rebellious siblings. Or, worst of all, spiritual retrenchment and resentment toward our Maker.

We have a choice. We can lapse into a counterproductive, secular, "fight or flee" point of view — and do a continual "slow burn." Such a perspective leads to indulgent self-pity, seething anger, or anguishing depression. A feeling of being victimized!

Or, we can see boulders on our trails as *"stepping stones,"* not "stumbling blocks." We can recast setbacks as *helps* rather than hindrances; *opportunities* not oppressions; *"lemonade ingredients"* instead of just "sour fruit."

But, to be a bit more specific, what lessons can we profitably digest from the wilderness experiences described above? Lessons that inform us as we negotiate our own? Norm clues us in.

First, let's focus on the *landscape*. We might as well not delude ourselves. Fantasy is for children, the deranged, and persons engrossed in denial. We might as well "face the music," and that means accepting the fact that the landscape of the wilderness is always harsh, and incredibly challenging.

It can be, and often is, a place that is:

➤ *unfamiliar:* strange, unfamiliar turf, away from life's "comfort zone";

➤ *lonely:* where we feel abandoned, orphaned, exiled — because someone is missing;

➤ *deprived:* affirmations are stripped away, so that we feel insignificant, alienated — because *something* is absent.

➤ *transitional:* with no end in sight, stability is nonexistent, and we can only anticipate ongoing calamity.

If this were the sum-total of life's wilderness events, we would be without hope. But, fortunately, the Bible weaves a spiritual dimension into even the most traumatic scenario.

Second, it's time to zero in on the *Lord's scope.* To learn His lessons is to provide us with spiritual shock absorbers, positive attitudes, constructive growth, and confident obedience. Maybe, our journey will not be a lot easier, but it's guaranteed to be much more tolerable and infinitely more significant.

Now for the lessons.

First, the wilderness is an ideal location to examine, and cultivate, true holiness. Away from the clutter and clatter. Apart from obligation, responsibility, and enforced conformity. When disengaged from the "rut" of normal living, our minds can be freed up — our hearts can be sensitized, our spirits can be attuned, to His Spirit.

Is it any wonder that saints, through the ages, have retreated to the desert? There, they have experienced visions of God, received heavenly instruction and prayed intensely. Retreatists? Not hardly. Rather, for the most part, people who thirst for more of the Master's presence. Persons who desire to be equipped and enabled!

The crucial point is this: Rather than life's wildernesses being places of Divine *punishment,* as is so often concluded, they must be seen as locations for *preparation.* For authentic spiritual formation.

As one rightly put it: "He doesn't take us to the wilderness, life does." But, once there, He intends to maximize the experience.

Why? So that growth results, rather than extreme frustration. So that, upon our re-entry into life's congestion, we can be the *"light"* (Matt. 5:16), *"salt"* (Matt. 5:13) and *"leaven"* (Luke 13:21) — bringing illumination, purification, and lift.

Although we've been smack-dab in the wilderness, we exit it with less of the "wilderness" in us!

Second, in the wilderness, we can be acutely sensitized to things we have taken for granted. Things we have neglected or overlooked — to our detriment. Things like:

> ➤ *prayer:* People who really know prayer's power, and pray effectively have, almost without exception, derived these by taking "Wilderness 101."

> ➤ *relationships:* The *L.A. Times* has a slogan: "We're there for you every morning." After a lonely stint in the bleak wilderness, we'll declare the same to those around us.

> ➤ *ministry:* Having agonized in the desert, we'll feel a special call to "bind wounds," and lovingly offer His perspective, to those who are stuck.

> ➤ *solitude:* Most important, we see that "aloneness" need not mean loneliness. Jesus is there! Especially when we're alone.[13]

Incredibly valuable lessons from life's "boot camp!"

Lessons that will prepare us for battles requiring our best (cf. 2 Tim. 2:3-4). Lessons that will cause us to focus decreasingly on our unpleasant, wilderness

---

13. Extrapolated from Norm Shoemaker's message, entitled, "It Only Takes One — I Am the One," 32nd Annual Laymen's Retreat, Los Angeles District Church of the Nazarene, October 24, 1992.

place. Instead, we'll rivet our attention on a *person* (correction, *the* Person), Jesus Christ — just as *every* Book in the Bible has done (cf. Appendix E).

He alone makes our wilderness into a Promised Land! A place where we'll experience authentic, spiritual formation. Where our perspective will be corrected, enhanced, deepened — enabling us to cope.

If It Walks and Talks Like a Duck . . .

My mind was befuddled. My heart was broken. My future seemed as clear as the July, smoggy L.A. skyline. It was a rag-tag state of affairs. Then, at my very lowest point, Jesus offered a new perspective. What had seemed discouraging, and even hopeless, was no longer. And I owe it all to Him.

Did my situation qualify as a bona fide "wilderness" experience? If the term implies outer bleakness, coupled with inner torment, count me in as a legitimate specimen. I felt "the hot sand of adversity" between my tender toes, and failed to spot anything that looked like an "oasis."

But, I hasten to say, after beginning to work through *that* wilderness, something startling occurred: I found myself better able to cope with any other kind of wilderness experience!

Negative circumstances, the so-called "blows of fate," no longer pummeled me into submission. Immune to pain? No way. Undiscourageable? You gotta' be kidding.

Rather, it all had to do with my coping mechanism. It became operable. A feeling emerged: There's nothing that God and I can't handle!

Strange thing. I hadn't ever requested God for "that feeling." All I wanted was help to rise above my

"Waterloo" experience. He took the initiative to go far beyond my simple request — equipping me with "new coronary eyes," and providing me with the means for coping with any kind of wilderness whatsoever!

Like all of us, I can only extrapolate from my own experience — like the fellow Jesus healed of blindness, who was hauled before cynical Pharisees. The latter exerted all kinds of pressure to get his admission that Jesus was a sinner. His answer: *"One thing I do know. I was blind but now I see"* (John 9:25).

To his testimony, I can only say "Amen" and "ditto."

And the same is, no doubt, true for scores of us. We could join in a chorus or symphony of "Amens." And we will someday, won't we!

Well, we've explored one unexpected, bonus blessing from having our perspective squared away. And that's not all. Not by a long shot.

Let's turn the crank on our huge spotlight, and beam rays of light on God's second big surprise.

Spare God A Moment

But, what's our rush? We would do ourselves a big favor to pause and do some heavy-duty reflecting on a few crucial issues. Issues that we've been exploring with our minds and hearts.

1. **What are some "wilderness experiences" I've had to go through? How have I thought of these? Minor in number and intensity? More than "my share?" Payback for undeserved blessings or personal sins?**

2. Have I ever second-guessed, or "nagged," God for having to suffer through "wilderness experiences?" If not, what stopped me from doing it? If so, what underlying thoughts prompted me?

3. What Christian viewpoints have been given to me, which have helped me cope (and even grow) through "wilderness experiences?" (Write them out. Then pause to thank God for them.)

CHAPTER THIRTEEN

The "People Thing"

*"By expressing appreciation,
we make excellence in others our property."*
(Voltaire)

*"God never gives us discernment that we may criticize,
but that we may intercede."*
(Oswald Chambers)

"Write your injuries in dust, and your benefits in marble."
(Charles Swindoll)

"HELLO, WELCOME TO THE PSYCHIATRIC HOTLINE.

IF YOU ARE OBSESSIVE-COMPULSIVE, PLEASE PRESS 1
REPEATEDLY.

IF YOU ARE CO-DEPENDENT, PLEASE ASK SOMEONE TO
PRESS 2.

IF YOU HAVE MULTIPLE PERSONALITIES, PLEASE PRESS
3,4,5 and 6.

IF YOU ARE PARANOID-DELUSIONAL, WE KNOW WHO YOU
ARE AND WHAT YOU WANT. JUST STAY ON THE LINE SO
WE CAN TRACE THE CALL.

IF YOU ARE SCHIZOPHRENIC, LISTEN CAREFULLY AND A
LITTLE VOICE WILL TELL YOU WHAT NUMBER TO
PRESS.

IF YOU ARE MANIC-DEPRESSIVE, IT DOESN'T MATTER
WHICH NUMBER YOU PRESS. NO ONE WILL ANSWER!"[1]

---

1. Heard on Los Angeles radio station KABC, the "Ken and
Barclay, Incorporated" morning program, September 12, 1995.

We Californians get ribbed a lot. We're reputed to be "touchy-feely" weirdos, who go around psychobabbling like crazy, and paying beaucoup bucks to our psychiatrists.

Not really. Not by a long shot. Granted, we may be a touch weird, but not the "basket cases" that our press proclaims. We're pretty much like folks in Boston, Birmingham or Billings: paying bills, raising children, watching too much TV, and trying to cope with our neighbors.

And like the rest of the planet, the last of these seems to challenge us the most. Getting along, as we're going along, eludes many sectors of our sun-drenched cities. Races riot, families abuse, and criminals prey. In short, we have ourselves a bona fide war zone!

But, we're not alone. Strife plagues the globe. In a very real sense, it always has. Historians inform us that there are only 200 years of recorded history, in which all wars ceased. Times when true *shalom* ruled.

Nevertheless, it seems like today's unrest rivals all previous periods. Not so much between nations, but between groups and persons. Even ones who perceive themselves to be good and decent, in:

> ➤ churches (There's an epidemic of church splits.);
> ➤ families (Abuse is now the #1 child killer.);
> ➤ occupations (Beware of your local postal worker!);
> ➤ organizations (Talked to a national militia guy lately?)

A lot of us concur with the small child who prayed:

"Dear God, please make all the bad people good and all the good people nice."

It is evident to me, as a social scientist, that three

dominant emotions possess our citizens today: fear, anger and detachment. And how are we responding?

*To **fear**, we become protective.* The security business is profiteering like mad. Cameras are trained, alarms are set, pistols are packed. But these only seem to intensify our paranoia. Over a third of us refuse to take walks around our own blocks! Protective? You bet.

*To **anger**, we become punitive.* Bring on the "Three-strikes Laws." Put those suckers away — forever. (We have 1.5 million in prison, and for each prisoner, the cost surpasses tuition costs at the most expensive Ivy League college!) Still, such intensified incarceration makes us feel better. We say: "Streets are safer; criminals are getting their just deserts."

*To **detachment**, we become desperate "joiners."* "Joiners" hook up with any groups that seem accepting, e.g., Weight Watchers, religious cults, volunteer organizations (e.g., animal rights), coffee klatches (Checked out the "groupies" at a Starbucks lately?), therapy groups. Togetherness is what counts, for it anesthetizes our pangs of loneliness.

I couldn't help smiling after hearing about some grown men meeting together for "12-step" therapy. Their purpose? To deal with agony they shared: when children, their mothers tossed away their baseball cards — worth tens of thousands today!

The responses we see to fear, anger, and detachment prompt many of us to long for those "good old days." But, others of us choose to face up to the challenges with vision and courage. To give it our very best shot.

As followers of the One who never evaded nor avoided, we must convince ourselves to take the road

He traveled.[2] To be sure, we'll never be completely immune from these dominant emotions — but, we must never allow them to bury us!

God's Word is our oasis, life support system and parachute, all rolled into one. Need a sampling of evidence? Bring on the three giant dragons, one by one, for a brief skirmish.

Fear? Paul tells Timothy: *"For God hath not given us the spirit of fear; but of power, and of love, and of a sound mind"* (2 Tim. 1:7, KJV). Similarly, the writer of Hebrews declares: *"The Lord is my helper; I will not be afraid. What can man do to me"* (Heb. 13:6)?

Anger, accompanied by an obsession to retaliate? Sorry. Not in our biblical role description! Romans 12:19 is emphatic: *"Do not take revenge . . . but leave room for God's wrath, for it is written: 'It is mine to avenge, I will repay, says the Lord.'"*

Detachment? That's a "no brainer." Hebrews instructs: *"God has said, 'Never will I leave you; never will I forsake you'"* (13:5).

Of course, we do more than give mental assent to these assurances. As Larry Cobb's provocative book affirms, we know them from the "inside out."[3] God's Spirit communicates them to the deepest recesses of our heart, so that its "eyes" become enlightened. So that we

---

2. See Jon Johnston, *Courage: You Can Stand Strong in the Face of Fear* (Grand Rapids: Victor Books, 1990).

The author discusses five levels of courage, ranging in gradation from less to more valuable: *fortitude, bravery, valor, resoluteness* and *chivalry*. The best of chivalry is exemplified in our "Holy Knight," Jesus. Finally, key ways that courage can be manifested today are discussed.

3. See Larry Cobb, *Real Change Is Possible — If You're Willing to Start From the Inside Out* (Colorado Springs: NavPress, 1988), pp. 219f.

possess an authentic, reliable Christian point of view.

But, in coping with our sick emotional environment, are there any suggestions for giving us strength and direction? Tips for helping us to keep our eyes clear and focused? Absolutely.

Let's begin on a positive note, focusing on persons who have responded to God's grace in an exemplary manner.

Locating Underground Springs

It's exciting for us to explore a picturesque California desert, and safe too — provided we know locations of water. Dehydration can "do a number" on our bodies in minutes. We can become "human tea kettles."

_____

Cobb underscores a valuable truth: "Nothing matters more for the Christian than walking the path that leads to knowing God. Knowing God changes us into richer, stronger, more loving Christians."

But, then he rhetorically asks: "(But I). . .wonder if such a path exists. There are paths to doctrinal knowledge, clean living, evangelistic fervor, disciplined conformity, and agreeable sociability, but is there really a path to knowing God so richly that our insides are changed?"

He proceeds to offer three reasons why he refuses to lose hope in his quest for inside-out change:

➤ *Scripture:* "The Bible points consistently to the possibility of knowing a God who delights in our fellowship and touches us with transforming power, e.g., Moses knew God face-to-face and was revolutionized."

➤ *Holy Spirit:* "(He) . . . has demonstrated His ability to penetrate my soul with ruthless exposure of all that I am and then to comfort and encourage, convict or prod."

➤ *Certain People:* "Several friends have deeply encouraged me with their integrity. I sense the reality of God when I'm with them. When they speak, the words come from deep parts of their souls." (more)

In a very real sense, we're all living in a kind of desert today. The penetrating sun of evil benumbs our mind. Burning sands of adversity scorch our spirit. We even run into a few circling buzzards, licking their chops, with obvious intentions!

The whole environment seems so alien: strange noises, startling sights. We almost feel like intruders, perhaps even spies. Nevertheless, our excursions continue, as we take it all in. As we keep tromping along.

But, from time to time, we're in need of water. It's imperative that we reinvigorate ourselves with refreshment and nourishment. Then, and only then, we'll be able to carry on.

What are the deep wells we draw from? Besides God's Word and His Holy Spirit? Answer: Persons who have hearts that are especially enlightened by Him. True servants of the King.

The author states that we must begin with an honest look — guaranteed to produce *confusion* (about what we see in our world and ourselves), cause *disappointment* (in others, often at critical moments) and provoke *conviction* (over the ways we violate the command to love).

Confusion, disappointment and conviction. How could they be the first steps to inner joy and a truly Christian perspective? Answer: If these are from God, they will inevitably promote the character of Christ within us.

More specifically, paraphrasing the author: **Confusion** *should lead to faith* — not bitterness or disappointment. **Disappointment** *should drive us to hope.* If we remain aware of all our heart longs for, even when badly hurt, then the thought of one day being with Christ can become our passion. **Conviction** *can push us to deep repentance* that opens up a new dimension of love. The writer summarizes:

> "(The pathway entails) . . . commitment to replacing false certainty, pretended satisfaction, and smug spirituality with disturbing levels of confusion, disappointment, and conviction, which in turn create the opportunity to develop faith, hope, and love."

And where can we locate them? Several places.

We can purchase airfare to Calcutta and visit with Mother Teresa, as my friend Senator Mark Hatfield has done. On the way, we could stop off in Rome to audience with the Pope.

Closer home, we might trek to North Carolina and pay a call on Billy Graham — or to Colorado Springs and drop in on James Dobson. Unrealistic? Maybe.

Well, how about visiting "deep wells," in the form of writings? Books can, without a doubt, link us to lifegiving sustenance.

Having read through William Barclay's commentaries,[4] John Wesley's volumes,[5] Oswald Chambers'

---

4. Some of my favorite quotations of William Barclay, Scottish writer and preacher are:

"Mary had learned to forget the world's commonest prayer — 'Thy will be changed' and to pray the world's greatest prayer — 'Thy will be done.'"

"Love clings to Christ even when the intellect cannot understand."

"The first thing that Jesus does for everyone of us is to say: 'Child, God is not angry with you. Come home, and don't be afraid.'"

"The greatest argument for Christianity: a genuinely Christian life."

"One security against sin lies in our being shocked by it."

"Christianity is the religion of the open hand, the open heart, the open door."

"He became what we are to make us what He is."

"Christianity always separates us, but it separates us not for privilege, and self-glory, and pride, but for service, and humility and love for all men."

"We cannot at one and the same time show that we are clever and that Christ is wonderful."

"If we would travel far, we must travel light."

"There is continuity between the Old and New Testaments, but continuity that ends in consummation."

(Cf. William Barclay, *The Daily Study Bible*, Philadelphia: The Westminster Press, 1956).

5. Some of my favorite quotations of John Wesley, eighteenth-century Reformation leader and founder of the Methodist Church, are:

works,[6] as well the writings of present day favorites — Lewis Smedes, Tony Campolo and the two "Chucks," Colson and Swindoll — I can heartily attest to the value of connecting with inspired minds.

Nevertheless, many of us simply aren't readers. No time.

Anywhere else we might find deep wells? In actuality, they're all around us! No need to limit our focus on celebrity ministers and big-name writers. We can "reach right out and touch" some of God's greatest servants. Persons who incarnate His Word and Spirit; who walk their talk.

Here's the kicker: They're usually disguised as common people — wearing old jeans to mow their yard, stumbling out of bed to go make a living, caring for a bedfast spouse, praying intently in their morning devotions, giving a few bucks to the homeless fellow on the corner. Just regular guys and gals, but still extraordinary in their own way.

How can we sort out these unsuspected saints? No special formula. It seems to just happen. After we've responded to God's grace, and given our highest pri-

---

"If you escape the persecution, you escape the blessing."

"Only use the world, but enjoy God."

"You have (no) power which you do not stand in need of."

"Want nothing of godliness but the power; want nothing of religion but the Spirit."

"No man ever went to heaven alone; he must either find friends or make them."

6. Some favorite quotes by Oswald Chambers, English preacher, are:

"All fret is caused by calculating without God."

"God does not offer . . . over-coming life; (rather). . . He gives us life as we overcome."

"If we learn to worship God in the trying circumstances, He will alter them in two seconds when He chooses."

ority to becoming His servants — partnering with Him in redeeming (gracing) His world — we cultivate a kind of "spiritual radar."

This super-sensitive gift enables us to spontaneously beam in on other servants. On spiritual kinsmen, who share parentage with our Father. And who, incidentally, possess our same kind of radar.

Not only do we locate each other, we're drawn together (one in the bond of love), and mutually grow as we engage in worship — in the form of fellowship!

Make no mistake, we can draw like crazy from these wells. And the water is chock-full of incredible nutrients: Christ-centered values, perspectives for coping, affirmation and encouragement for tired spirits.

Many of us have, no doubt, been privileged to encounter some of these deep wells. Persons whose lives "scream" Christian character; whose words, often spoken in a casual, offhanded manner, reflect volumes of spiritual vision. Results: We're never quite the same.

Unbeknown to them, they help us to sharpen our perspective — so we hone in on God's essentials. So that we're better able to catch His drift.

I'd like to share a sampling of statements, made by saints I've encountered in the desert. These extraordinary "ordinary" folks gifted me with spiritual nourishment:

"Jesus is always enough." (B. Edgar Johnson)

"When you think of God, color Him Jesus." (Reuben Welch)

"View life from the standpoint of God rather than men, eternity rather than time, heaven rather than earth, and the cross rather than the bank." (Richard Taylor)

"Vision without action is a dream, but action without vision is a nightmare." (Keith Wright)

"He is no fool who exchanges that which he cannot keep for that which he cannot lose." (Stephen Nease)

"My goals, for the rest of my life, are to be: tolerant without compromise, obedient without being judgmental, and honest without being unkind." (Earl Lee)

"There is only one Guy who had the right to throw rocks — and He didn't — He just wrote in the dirt." (Fritz Ridenour)

These particular "wells" became available to me at moments I was the most "thirsty." When I was starting to get stuck. When my vision was becoming cloudy. When my "frame" was ceasing to enhance life's picture with beauty — or hope.

We've all started sliding into such predicaments. If our hearts are open and teachable, the saints around us can help us to get back on track. They can remind us of old truth in new ways. Ways that dramatically impact our spirits and motivate us to go forward in faith!

But, get ready for a statement that reflects a T.G.O. (terrific grasp of the obvious): Not all persons resource us with sustenance.

Some do quite the opposite. They're more apt to force-feed us with a bitter drink that makes us cringe, and sometimes, collapse. In their presence, we're prone to getting stuck. Hung up and bogged down — especially in our attitude. We've discussed that issue in previous chapters.

More specifically, how does our Christian perspective help us to relate to people in general? All kinds?

Those up close and distant. People of all stripes and colors — the devoted, defiant, different, disinterested?[7]

How does knowing about, and accepting, God's grace — as well as desiring to be His servant, make us "people persons?" Persons who go about thoroughly engaged in reconciliation?

Let's pry open the door of inquiry a crack.

In the Same House, but On Different Floors

Paul declared that Christ's death was foolishness to the Greeks, and a stumbling block to the Jews (1 Cor. 1:23).[8] Similarly, our Lord's instruction on how His followers must relate to others defies the logic of today's secular world. Ted Engstrom lays the sharply contrasting viewpoints on the line:

---

7. See Jon Johnston, *Walls or Bridges: How to Build Relationships that Glorify God* (Grand Rapids: Baker Book House, 1985).

In this work, it is the author's basic contention that we meet four basic personality types in this world. They are:
- persons who are *devoted* to us;
- individuals who are *defiant* of us;
- people who are, simply, *different* from us; and,
- those who are *distant* from us.

Furthermore, it is our biblical mandate to "knock down walls" and "build bridges" between us. In order to do so, we must be able to understand each kind. Finally, with God's help, we must implement four distinct strategies to maximize our relationships (i.e., build bridges).

8. *"foolishness"* (Cf. 1 Cor. 1:22-25)

Jews thought the Good News of Jesus was "foolish." Why? They had been taught the Messiah would be a conquering king, who would restore David's throne — not a suffering servant. Also, a Savior could never be executed as a common criminal.

Greeks, likewise, considered the gospel "foolish." They disbelieved in a bodily resurrection; did not see in Jesus the powerful

NONCHRISTIAN VIEWPOINT	CHRISTIAN VIEWPOINT
◆ exploit the vulnerable masses	◆ befriend the poor, sick, etc.
◆ despise enemies — strike back, get revenge, stay mad	◆ love attackers — return good for evil, forgive, serve
◆ gain, and conspicuously display riches, so others will envy	◆ aspire for intangible treasures, stored in heaven[9]

As Engstrom declares, *we'll respond with compassion toward all who are weak and oppressed — orphans, widows, impoverished, lonely.* And we'll make very certain that we aren't, actively or passively, their oppressors. Period. Exclamation point!

Second, we'll return good for evil. Even though our "other cheek" turns black-and-blue. Recall what God said about judging and extracting vengeance. No way José. For a refresher course all we need do is check

---

characteristics of their mythological gods, and, like Jews, believed no reputable person would be crucified. [i.e., Death, itself, implied defeat — never victory.]

"stumblingblock" (Cf. Rom. 9:31-33).

According to Paul, Israel pursued salvation by works (a law of righteousness), not by faith. Thus, they stumbled over the "Stumbling Stone" (i.e., Jesus), for He didn't meet their messianic expectations.

Today, many stumble over Christ because:

➤ Salvation *by faith* doesn't make sense to many.

➤ Other expect Him to, simply, *overlook their shortcomings.*

➤ Still others stumble because *His values oppose the world's.* (He asks for humility, not success, and many are unwilling to humble themselves before Him.)

➤ Finally, scores stumble because they *refuse to acknowledge any authority or lordship.* They want control.

(*Life Application Bible: New Testament* [The Living Bible] Wheaton, IL: Tyndale House Publishers, Inc., 1987, p. 421.)

9. Ted Engstrom, *The Fine Art of Friendship: Building and Maintaining Quality Relationships* (Nashville: Thomas Nelson Publishers, 1985), pp. 125-126.

out Christ's "Sermon on the Mount" (Matthew 5-7).

Finally, our lives will model simplicity rather than materialism, frugality more than ostentatiousness, compassion not selfishness. In short, we're to be His exhibits to the world — showcasing His perspective to the world. Paul captures the point with these straightforward words:

> *"Do nothing out of selfish ambition or vain conceit, but in humility consider others better than yourselves. Each of you should look not only to your own interests, but also to the interests of others"* (Phil. 2:3-4)

But, for a moment, let's focus on a special category of persons that increasingly surround us. Specifically, those who make no pretense of sharing our Christian viewpoint. The pagans, who breathe God's air, and are oblivious (or obstinate) to biblical truth.

How must we relate to them in a servantile manner? Now that's a sticky wicket!

At times, they're at each others' throats. And we have every reason under the sun to remain uninvolved — except one: We're Christians. That makes us involved automatically.

We need only ask my friend and Christian colleague at Pepperdine, Stan Moore. His unforgettable story illustrates Christian involvement to a "T." Incidentally, Hollywood might even be interested in this plot — after all, it contains violence and nudity!

A "Boxer" Rebellion

Stan attended Wheaton College near Chicago, and became acquainted with Dick Gleason. He was minister of the South Side Christian Center — a place that caringly reached out to neglected, delinquency-prone youth.

One day, Dick rushed in to tell Stan that he had heard about an upcoming "gang rumble." Furthermore, he knew *when* it was planned and even *where* it would occur.

He explained that he had attempted to phone the police "hot line," but received zilch response. Then, in panic, he motioned for Stan to quickly jump in his car. Together, they raced to the scene.

There, sure enough, two gangs were about to clash in the middle of a vacant lot. Approximately 200 fellows were on each side, armed with chains, clubs, metal rods and guns. Almost as many girls cheered them on.

Suddenly, on impulse, Dick did something very strange. He began ripping off his clothes. In a split second, off came his clerical collar, shirt, pants — until all he had on was his boxers. Then he yelled at the top of his lungs:

> "Wait! Stop! Look at me! I know I look stupid, But, I don't look half as crazy as you — ready to kill one another in cold blood! Why not choose one from each of your gangs to fight it out!?" [Recalling the "David and Goliath" story came in handy!]

The fellows froze in their tracks. The nearly naked "lunatic" had captured their attention. Furthermore, he had offered an alternative to massive bloodshed.

Both sides chose their strongest "honchos." These two guys grabbed their chains, metal rods, and the rest of their "hospitality kit." The battle began. Only one triumphed that day. The vanquished had to be rushed, by ambulance, to the emergency room of a nearby hospital.

Although a heavy price was paid, a far greater tragedy had been averted — thanks to the quick, unconventional tactics of Dick Gleason. His intrusion, into a very hostile environment, bought life-saving time.

Intervention between warring parties. A legitimate, advisable part of our Christian role description? Absolutely — but always with discretion. We must be prompted, and counseled, by God's Spirit within.

But, how about when defiant "predators" come after us? When we're the planned main course for their next big meal?

This truth is absolute: At no better time do we reveal our Christlikeness than when attacked. Remember how throngs in His hometown, Nazareth, sought to cast Him off a cliff? How Roman soldiers came, armed to the teeth, to arrest Him at Gethsemane? Hear His words: *"If the world hates you, keep in mind that it hated me first. . . . If they persecuted me, they will persecute you also"* (John 15:18, 20).

Sometimes, our most frustrating "persecution" can take the form of non-response. There can be a total disregard and disinterest — as in the days of Noah. When we're in the vicinity, persons just push the "turn-off" button, and we're "tuned out." The wall goes up. The gate is locked.

To both forms of persecution, what must our response be?

Our Very Best "Curb Appeal"

In a powerful CHRISTIANITY TODAY editorial, Charles Colson evaluates ways that Christians seek to influence our sinful culture.

First, we infiltrate politics — "seeking justice, defending the unborn, fighting for the family." Very worthwhile indeed! But, such activism has its limits. Why? Because many of today's vexing problems defy political solution. Furthermore, the media has equated Christianity with a distorted image of the Religious Right. Result? "(O)ur political voice is made to drown-out our prophetic voice."

Second, with logical, persuasive argument, we defend our Christian worldview against others in our culture. That's as it should be. Solid, rational, apologetics is desperately needed. But, like the first, this approach is limited. Hear Colson's poignant words:

"No matter how coherent our message, it won't take root unless it resonates with our listeners' own experiences, which today are less and less attuned to the gospel."

What, then, is our best approach? According to the author, there's one primary way people will genuinely "see" the gospel message: *By observing how we lovingly relate together as Christians.*[10]

To illustrate, Chuck told about a P.B.S. interview. The interviewer seemed hard-boiled and no-nonsense. Her first question was sarcastic: "How can you be so sure about your faith?" Without hesitation, Colson began telling a story of his time behind bars after Watergate.

---

10. Charles Colson, *Christianity Today*, "Wanted: Christians Who Love," Oct. 2, 1995, p. 112.

A favorite fable of Ted Engstrom is "the devil's clearance sale." Satan is standing before a big table of tools: the sword of jealousy, the knife of fear, and the hangman's noose of hatred. Just about every tool in Satan's possession was for sale — at

Many Christians reached out to him in love, but none more than Al Quie (sixth-ranking Republican in the House). One day he called to say: "Chuck, because of your family problems, I'm going to ask the President if you can go home, while I serve the rest of your prison term." Risking an entire political career because of love?! What a convincing witness that Jesus is real!

Well, as our friend retold the story for the cameras, the interviewer suddenly broke down, waved her hand, and said: "Stop, stop!" A mixture of tears and mascara streamed down her face. She dashed to her dressing room to regain composure and repair her makeup.

After her return, the cameras rolled again. But, again, Chuck's story caused her to "lose it completely."

Finally, the footage was completed. But the interviewer softly admitted to being greatly impacted. In fact, she was touched so deeply, that she vowed to return to the church she had abandoned years earlier.

The point is unmistakably clear: *"A Christian community united in love attracts attention in the most jaded culture."*

To underscore his point, Mr. Colson tosses in this quote by Alasdair MacIntyre (*Difficulties in Christian Belief*):

---

very high prices.

Standing alone on an ornately carved wooden pedestal was a worn, battered wedge — the devil's most used and prized possession. He used it to wedge division between Christians. It was the only tool he needed to stay in business. And it wasn't for sale! (Ibid., p.122).

Where the Christian community is incapable of
producing lives such as those of the saints, the
premises from which it argues will appear root-
less and arbitrary.[11]

As His servants, we'll do our utmost to express
love to other believers. That's a "given," just like a
theorem we memorized in high school geometry class.

Why? Because our cynical world is looking on, and
desperately needs to see faith in action. Also, because
we share the same Christian point of view.

One more reason: the Bible tells us to. In John 13
and 17, our Lord's bottom line is: Be visibly united in
love. Love that resonates with our deepest longings
— and points to our loving God.

Paul drives home the same scriptural nail: "*... make
my joy complete by being like-minded, having the
same love, being one in spirit and purpose*" (Phil. 2:2)

Peter weighs in with: "*Finally, all of you, live in
harmony with one another, be sympathetic, love as
brothers*" (1 Pet. 3:8)

John supplies the capper: "*We know that we have
passed from death to life, because we love our
brothers*" (1 John 3:14).

It should be a snap for us. That is, if "those other
Christians" return the favor. If they're as devoted to
servanthood as we are.

Unfortunately, once again, this doesn't always
occur. At times, it's quite difficult for us to distinguish
the Christians from the lions!

But, regardless of others' reactions, we must
remain consistent. And what should our consistency
consist of? Paul provides us with a Christ-centered

---

11. Colson, p. 112.

agenda that includes this unbeatable "trilogy" (Rom. 12:12):

1. joyful in hope;

2. patient in affliction; and,

3. faithful in prayer.

If only we'd start each day by affirming these marvelous manifestations of our Christian point of view! Our days would go better. Our pagan compatriots might be forced to do some deep, introspective soul-searching. Our verbal, and nonverbal, testimony would ring true.

As servants of the King, can we do less?

Another Quick Pause

We've explored two spin-off, spill-over dividends that accompany our Christian point of view.

First, adverse circumstances won't "sink our clock."

Second, we'll draw strength from other Christians. Like grapes from the same Vine (John 15:5).

Also, we'll become increasingly equipped to relate more effectively with others. Whether they're needy, obstinate, distant or downright pagan.

But, how about benefits to ourselves? What can this marvelous Christian frame of reference do for our self-concept? Our self-acceptance and respect?

It is to this "hot" cultural issue that we now turn, but from an angle that contrasts with the world's.

But, once again, before scurrying on — shall we do the "glance-over-the-shoulder" bit again. Let's take time to carefully, and prayerfully, reflect of these questions:

1. Which of these "deep wells" have I drawn from?
   A. High profile ministers (up close or at a distance);
   B. Christian writers;
   C. Saints nearby.
   [Also, what wisdom and/or inspiration did each contribute to my life? To what extend did each help me at "just the right time"?]

2. How have I noticed widespread fear, anger and detachment in those around me? To what degree have these emotions impacted me? In what ways have my typical responses reflected an authentic Christian point of view?

3. Do I believe that our world is becoming increasingly pagan? What is my evidence? Is Mr. Colson correct in declaring that my best witness consists of showing genuine love to other Christians?

CHAPTER FOURTEEN

The Source of My Shadow

"When Nature leaves a hole in a person's mind,
she usually plasters it over with conceit."
(Henry Wadsworth Longfellow)

"We don't see the world as it is, we see it as we are."
(Anaïs Nin)

"The one nice thing about being imperfect
is the joy it brings to others."
(Doug Larson)

Harold Morowitz received one of those "loving insult" birthday cards we've all seen. This one declared that the materials making up his body are worth only 97 cents!

The Yale scientist decided to have some fun. Using a biochemical catalog, he priced-out the various ingredients of his body. Here are some per-gram values he discovered:

- hemoglobin($2.95)
- acetate kinase($8,860)
- follicle-stimulating hormone($4,800,000)
- prolactin($17,500,000)

Morowitz arrived at $245.54 as the average per-gram-dry-weight market value of his body. Since his 168 pounds (76,364 grams) is sixty-eight percent water, his dry weight is 24,436 grams. Multiplying that by $245.54 per gram, he calculates that he is worth $6,000,015.44. A six million dollar man, and he's not even bionic!

That's not all. If his human constituents are synthesized from simpler to more complex forms, his estimated worth jumps to six billion dollars. Ready for this? If his body components are assembled into cells, Morowitz maintains that his price tag tops out at a mind-boggling 6,000 trillion dollars.[1]

Finally, he asks the most crucial question of all: How are his cells assembled into tissues, tissues into organs, and organs into the great guy known as Harold Morowitz? The task staggers our imagination. Dollar values suddenly become irrelevant.

The conclusion to all of this seems so self-evident: *We are all priceless.* Every last one of us. Worth more than the Queen's Crown Jewels! More than all this world's real estate combined!

Nevertheless, so many seem to ignore, or even contest, this conclusion. Criminals are branded. Homeless are labeled. Unattractive are shunned. Poor are harshly judged. Aged are relegated. Sick are thought burdensome. Eccentric are ignored. Oh yes, lest we forget, the unborn are considered inhuman and expendable.

Why? Because many are afflicted with a sin-dominated perspective. To use Christ's metaphor, a huge "plank" blocks out clear vision (Matt. 7:6). Charles Swindoll isn't "whistlin' Dixie" when he declares: "Sin blinds; sin binds; and, sin grinds."[2]

---

1. Phillip Morrison, in editorial entitled "How Much Are You Worth," (*Twenty-First Century Christian*, date unknown, p. 3), quotes data in *Hospital Practice* by Harold J. Morowitz.

2. Charles R. Swindoll, *Living Above the Level of Mediocrity:*

Result? Many of us are evaluated on the basis of unchristian, bogus criteria, like: bucks, buddies, looks, clout, blood.

Saddest of all, scores of us victimize *ourselves* by accepting the world's insulting evaluation scheme carte blanche. We reason: "Who are we to refute their overwhelming negative feedback?"[3]

But this cannot be. It is imperative that we replace any nagging sense of low self-esteem with one that is accurate and healthy. One that is characterized by plenty of:

> ➤ *self-acceptance* (seeing clearly who we are);
> ➤ *self-approval* (living comfortably with who we are);
> ➤ *self-affection* (being grateful for who we are).

But, for starters, it is advisable for us to do a quick self-analysis.

Telltale Evidence

Just as a sore, raspy throat can suggest the presence of cold germs, and a clanky automobile engine

---

A Commitment to Excellence (Waco, TX: Word Books, 1987), p. 270.

3. Sociologist Charles Horton Cooley coined the term, "looking glass self," to explain the effects of society on our self-appraisal. He writes: "Self and society are twin-born." (*Social Organization*, New York: Schocken, 1962, p. 5).

In another book he elaborates:

"As we see our face, figure, and dress in the glass, and are interested in them because they are ours, and pleased or otherwise with them according as they do or do not answer to what we would like them to be, so in imagination we perceive in another's mind some thoughts of our appearance, manners, aims, deeds, character, friends, and so on, and are variously affected by it." (*Human Nature And The Social Order*, New York: Schocken, 1964, p. 184).

can signal an insufficient quantity of oil, so certain key symptoms strongly indicate that our self-esteem has "tanked."

At the offset, we must remind ourselves that most of these indicators, periodically, surface in all of our lives. That's par for our human course. It's only when they are excessive in intensity and duration that we should be seriously concerned. With that qualification in mind, it's onward to the symptoms:

1. Incessant craving for positive evaluations from others.

If we're afflicted by this serious malady we'll resort to such things as voicing insincere compliments or faking compliance. Why? To evoke "strokes" from those who, because of our actions, feel "obligated" to reciprocate.

We become super-sensitive to others' feedback — like a *thermometer* that constantly picks up external cues — to obtain our self-worth readouts.

By contrast, if we regard ourselves as intrinsically worthwhile, we're neither made heady by compliment nor devastated by insult. Our course is steady and our spirit remains confident.

We're more apt to resemble a *thermostat* that controls (not merely registers) life's temperature.

2. Primarily propelled into action by such negative factors as fear, guilt and crisis.

When our self-image shrinks, the "I-can-do-it" feeling invariably subsides. As a result, innovation, creativity and ambition fade. We become devoid of energy and courage; our vision becomes clouded by a fear that makes unfamiliar thought and behavior patterns seem threatening.

Overtaken by such a condition, it is little wonder

why we often lack a self-starter and lapse into apathy.

Some of us may only become responsible marital partners, when pressured by the threat of divorce. Others of us might stop overeating, after we've had a heart attack. Still others of us may cease driving recklessly, after having a terrible accident.

By sharp contrast, when we have a healthy self-image we tend to be "actors" rather than "reactors." We choose to mold, rather than being molded by, our environment. To paraphrase Huxley, we do *what* needs to be done, *when* it ought to be done, *as* it should be done, *whether* we enjoy doing it or not. Our inner aliveness provides our springboard for action!

3. Unwilling, or perhaps even unable, to give.

Giving, whether in the form of money or love, entails the relinquishment of resources, and even becoming more vulnerable to the recipient.

Those of us with a starved self-image find it very difficult to cultivate a generous spirit. We reason: Anybody we give to will be that much better off, and we'll be that much poorer. Why not out-earn and out-accumulate others? In so doing, we'll convince ourselves, and everyone else, of our worth!

Buying into this perspective, we are likely to relate to others in one (or more) of these manipulative ways:

> ➤ put them down — "You are beneath me and my kind."
> ➤ put them on — "I'll only disclose what I want you to see."
> ➤ put them off — "I'll avoid an authentic relationship with you."[4]

---

4. The underlying assumption is superiority, accompanied by incessant self-applause. This frequently results in contempt for

Obviously, when we resort to such tactics, people are sure to not be warmly receptive. Instead, they're likely to respond with negative feedback that only intensifies our self-hatred.

It is so ironic. By insisting on getting rather than giving, we deny ourselves of the very antidote necessary for improving our self-esteem. My dad's old adage is right after all: If we sprinkle the perfume of generosity upon others, we're bound to spill a few drops of self-respect upon ourselves. Jesus declared, and demonstrated so convincingly: *"It is more blessed to give than to receive"* (Acts 20:35).

4. Overly defensive.

If we doubt our self-worth, we're apt to be excessively protective. The walls of our psychic castle are

---

us "lesser mortals." They figure, according to Engstrom, "There's no need for road manners if you're a fifteen-ton truck!" (Ted Engstrom, *The Fine Art of Friendship: Building and Maintaining Quality Relationships.* New York: Thomas Nelson Publishers, 1985, p. 105).

Cf. David G. Myers, *The Inflated Self: Human Illusions and the Biblical Call to Hope* (New York: The Seabury Press, 1980). Award-winning research psychologist, Myers, surveys a fascinating array of experimental studies that demonstrate how the *superiority complex*, rather than low self-esteem, is at the root of most persons' distorted images of themselves.

The evidence from these studies joins hands with the biblical understanding of human nature and behavior that sees them as self-delusions issuing from an inflated and inaccurate sense of self. But the author argues that theological concepts like "sin" and "guilt," which the empirical literature cannot use, points to the deeper origin of such syndromes.

Delivered originally as the Finch Lectures at Fuller Theological Seminary, Professor Myers reflects on the often grisly, often amusing foibles of thinking and judgment that issue from the "self-serving bias" in its many guises. (book fly leaf)

high and thick, and our guns are trigger-ready to blast away at any perceived hint of encroachment.

Our weapons are many: argument, insult, rejection through body language, and even emotional withholding (e.g., "silent treatment").

Such tactics are thought to be necessary for "holding off the enemy" at a safe distance. Should he get close, he might detect how weak and defenseless we really are. In effect, ours is a game of calculated bluff based on paranoia.

In addition, if we're haunted by self-doubt, we have an arsenal of weapons to protect ourselves from ourselves. These "defense mechanisms" function to protect us from the harsh (real or imagined) enemies of reality. Let's examine a few:

➤ **rationalization:** thinking up plausible explanations to excuse ourselves (*"But everyone cheats on their income taxes."*)

➤ **compensation:** stressing a strength to camouflage a weakness (*"So what if you saw me read a porno magazine. Don't overlook the fact that I read five versions of the Bible regularly."*)

➤ **projection:** attributing our own unacceptable attitudes or behavior to others (*"I'm sure you'll dislike him the way I do."*)

➤ **displacement:** venting aggressive feelings toward "safe" sources that aren't responsible for our plight (*"Whenever I get this upset at my boss, I kick the dog."*)

Although other defense mechanisms are common, we seem to employ these the most.

Once again, recall that the key word is "excessive." At times, we all need shock absorbers to help us absorb unbearable pain. Pain associated with being brutally rejected by a loved one, receiving shocking news about a terminal condition, failing to pass a crucial exam or receive a deserved promotion.

5. Getting tangled in the quagmire of pessimism and fatalism.

Carl Sandburg once said: "Life is like an onion. You take off one layer at a time, and sometimes you cry."

If we're a self-hater, we'll weep profusely. And our crying will intensify as we examine the deepest layers of our innermost selves. God, we fear, has made "junk" — and we are it.

With such perspective, it is little wonder that things seem bleak and joy is exterminated. Life, as Thomas Carlyle describes it, is little more than a "dreadful circle going around and around toward the hole in the sink."

Caught in this web, we lock our gaze upon the actual, and completely disregard the potential. According to us, our fate is as fixed as cement; we are born to lose. And the future only offers more of the same, or worse.

In addition, we become a drag on those with whom we work and live. In addition, we become barriers that block their creative achievement and self-improvement.

By contrast, if we feel good about ourselves, we'll direct our focus toward the positive. (Recall Seligman's principles in chapter 4). We'll describe our cup as "half full" rather than as "half empty." We'll focus on the dough, rather than the hole, in life's "doughnut."

With a smile that bespeaks of inner peace, we're apt to say something like: "Even a broken clock is right twice a day."[5] And we're right!

To say that we can get thoroughly stuck with a self-accusing, negative self-image is to state the obvious. Without a biblical viewpoint, our lives can reflect each of the five characteristics above. Furthermore, this can result in relationship impasses — roadblocks that we've created by not allowing God's Spirit to enlighten the eyes of our heart.

Key question: What difference is made by cultivating an authentic Christian perspective? How is our self-concept strengthened and informed?

It's Dividend Time Again!

As persons graced by God — co-laboring with Him in redeeming His world, considering ourselves His possession, we have legitimate right to feel great about our identity.

His Son and our Lord, Jesus, spilled His life's blood (Rom. 5:8) to provide us with a joy that transcends any temporary disappointment (John 15:11). And, as a huge bonus, we possess abundant life that is eternal (John 10:10)!

His Word describes us as His *"workmanship"* (Eph. 2:10). Allow the full impact of that thought to sink in our minds. The divine Creator considers us His masterpiece — transcending even the incredible beauties of nature. And He proudly showcases us for a sinful and corrupt world to see. Exhibit A.

Why? Because of what His Son lovingly did on our behalf. We've been redeemed!

---

5. Excerpts extracted from *Building Self-Esteem* (Aldersgate Dialog series), Gene Van Note, ed., chapter 2 entitled, "Symptoms of a Lack of Self-esteem," by Jon Johnston, Kansas City: Beacon Hill Press, pp. 16-21, n.d.

Once this great truth is grasped, our anemic self-image is nourished into new life. We're given a Divine fuel injection. Doubts are quelled. Inner striving ceases. We have deep and abiding rest.

Furthermore, responding as His servants, our motivations contrast with those who do not "see clearly." Those, according to Lewis Smedes, having hearts that are driven by three restless urges:

1. To feel good: satisfy a consuming hunger for pleasure-giving sensations.

Hear Smedes' insightful comment: "(Such) commitment to pleasant feelings is like a religious devotion: its sacred relics are the Valium bottle, the wine goblet and the self-help book. . . Anybody's favorite therapist is its high priest."[6]

2. To make good: get power, or a modest mint of money, be well known for at least a day, i.e., make "big."

Again, Smedes declares: For the success-driven, the hot investment counselor is its "prophet"; the stock exchange is its "high altar."

3. To look good: well-toned body draped in designer clothes, and topped with an attractive face; make a good impression.

The author states that such an individual intently listens for the ultimate "benediction": "You look fantastic!" And the health spa is its "wayside chapel."[7]

Feel good. Make good. Look good.

Not that these are "bad goods," they're just —

---

6. Lewis B. Smedes, *A Pretty Good Person: What It Takes to Live with Courage, Gratitude and Integrity or When Pretty Good Is as Good as You Can Be* (New York: Harper and Row, Publishers, 1990), p. 2.

7. Ibid.

according to Smedes — very "bad gods" — that "eventually leave us feeling like spent dreams." His conclusion: "They need to be planted in the (greatest good of all), namely, **being good**."[8]

Not to earn His favor (Eph. 2:8-9; Titus 3:5). Not to impress Him with intense devotion. (Recall Christ's reprimand of the Pharisees, who ostentatiously prayed on street corners?) Not dutifully, as something distasteful that's owed.

None of these. Instead, as a spontaneous act of worship springing forth from a servant's heart. A heart that is immensely grateful, and with a clear conscience. In a word, one that sees ever so clearly.

And that's what gives us self-esteem — from the inside out!

Robert S. McGee is right in declaring:

> Whether labeled *"self-esteem"* or *"self-worth,"* the feeling of significance is crucial to the emotional, spiritual and social stability of people. The need to believe we are significant is the driving element within the human spirit. Understanding this single need opens the door of understanding our actions and attitudes.[9]

The feeling of significance. That's the incredible, spin-off dividend we're gifted with when we possess Christian perspective!

Not arrogance. That's an affront to God. Not complete self-sufficiency, like the self-made man who "worships his maker." Our heavenly Father expects us

---

8. Ibid.

9. *Herald Of Holiness*, "Positive Self-esteem: Discovering Who I Am in Christ," by Ronald L. Phelps, August, 1992, p. 4. (Cf. Robert S. McGee, *The Search For Significance*, p. 13).

to lean hard on Him in utter dependency (1 Pet. 5:8).

The significance I speak of takes place when God inhabits every "room" of our "house." A touching little story, told in *Guideposts*, illustrates my point.

It's Moving Day!

While my husband, a Presbyterian medical missionary, was still alive we were always traveling. Every place we went we received gifts from warmhearted people. There was one that I shall never forget.

In 1941, we stopped briefly in Manila while my husband visited a hospital. With the help of a young Filipino boy, I was shopping for some shells in the downtown area, but the prices were too high.

Disappointed, I had started back to the shop when the boy asked me to follow him. He moved through the crowded streets of Manila to the shabby home where he lived in poverty with his mother.

On the table in his room were the loveliest shells I had ever seen.

The boy pulled out a battered box and put the shells into it. He handed it to me.

"You know I haven't the money to pay for these," I said.

"Lady, I don't want you to pay for them," the dark-haired boy said, smiling, 'I want to give them to you!'

He had not asked me to select my favorite. He had not offered to give me half and keep half himself. He simply handed me *all*.

When I got back to the ship, I went to our little cabin, shut the door and sat on the edge of the bunk looking at the shells. I said to myself,

"Here I am, a missionary. I was raised in a Christian home. I was educated at a Christian college. I have known the Lord Jesus so long I cannot remember when I did not know Him. But I do not believe I have ever said to Him what that little boy said to me. 'Here, take all.'"

That night, in that darkened cabin aboard the creaking ship, for the first time, I gave Jesus Christ the keys to my life.

I gave Him the key to the library of my life, so that every book I read would be in conformity with His will. I gave Him the key to the living room, declaring I would never view anything or listen to anything that He did not want me to see or hear.

I gave Him the key to everything — to my diary, the closets, the attic, every secret place. I said, *"No longer will I be the host and You the guest in my house. The house is Yours and I shall be Your servant."*

So this is my prized possession: a battered box full of shells.[10]

Likewise, when we relinquish all to Him, and *"trust in the Lord with all our heart"* (Prov. 3:5-6) there is a rest that transcends all others. The strain and struggle cease. No need to "white-knuckle-it" through life any longer. Why? Because He is in complete control.

Then, and only then, will our lives have significance. And, in tandem with significance, will come the most satisfying sense of self-worth imaginable!

---

10. *Guideposts*, "Biggest Gift in the World: A Young Boy Teaches An Unforgettable Lesson in Giving," by Julia Lake Kellersberger, January, 1974, n.p.

And now we move to the final chapter, to share the ultimate dividend of our Christian perspective: Knowing God. No, I mean really knowing Him in His fullness, justice and love. But, before raising the curtain for our "Hallelujah Chorus," let's pause to reflect on these questions:

Taking a Moment to Apply Truth

1. In what ways would I describe myself? In doing this, is it evident what I consider my top priority(ies)?

2. Do I fall prey to any of the five "symptoms of poor self-esteem" mentioned? Which ones? Why these?

3. Am I more intent on feeling, making and/or looking good than being good? What is my evidence? Why am I this way?

4. Have I invited God to inhabit all the "rooms" of my "house?" Which ones are still under my control? Would I be willing to offer Him each of these right now?

CHAPTER FIFTEEN

Daring to Call Him "Daddy"

"When people cease believing in God,
they don't believe in nothing, but fall for anything."
(C.G. Chesterton)

"If you move but one step toward God,
you are not as other men are."
(John Wesley)

"If only God would give me a clear sign!
Like making a large deposit in my name at a Swiss bank."
(Woody Allen)

Wayne Dyer describes a conversation taking place between two *in utero* babies, confined to the wall of their mother's womb. One declares: "I know you're going to find this hard to accept, but I truly believe there is life after birth."

The other snaps back: "Don't be ridiculous. Look around. This is it. Make yourself comfortable and forget about this life-after-birth nonsense."

After a while the first pipes up again: "Don't get upset with me, but I believe there is a Mother."

"A Mother?! You're out of your mind! Just accept that this is all there is — no life after birth and, definitely, no Mother. Now grab hold of that cord and shut up!"

Baby #1 relaxes for a moment, but simply can't contain her restless thoughts: "I have only one more thing to say. Then, I promise, I'll never bug you again. Okay?"

With a disgusted look, her captive audience nods for her to hurry and get it over with.

"You know about those constant pressures we both feel. The continual movements and repositionings that make us so uncomfortable. Well, I've thought it through. It's going to get a lot worse.

"But, we must not fear. At the very moment when we think we can't stand any more. When our discomfort gets as intense as it can possibly get — something wonderful will happen. We will meet Mother face-to-face, and know ecstasy beyond anything we can possibly imagine!"[1]

Do these two viewpoints sound familiar? The conversation between these small fries represents two dominant viewpoints in our world: *theism* and *atheism*.

According to all polls I've seen, most of us are the first. Agreeing with over ninety percent of the natural scientists (e.g., Einstein, von Braun), we possess a deep, inner certitude that God exists.

Also, that He cares lots about every last (and lost) one of us!

But, undeniably, there are bona fide atheists — defined by one as "people having no invisible means of support," and by another as "persons who don't give a rip who wins the Notre Dame-S.M.U. football game."

Like the god Protaeus of Greek mythology, atheism assumes many forms. Charles Colson describes, perhaps, the most dominant one in another of his

---

1. Wayne W. Dyer, *Your Sacred Self: Making the Decision to Be Free* (New York: Harper Collins Publishers, 1995), pp. 1-2.

Christianity Today editorials. He terms it "New Age neo-paganism."

The secular media trumpets it loudly and continuously. Why? According to Colson, "Its emphasis on the 'autonomous self' squares neatly with the cultural elite's intellectual and moral relativism. . .Do-it-yourself God-kits pose no threat." There's no single Voice of Authority to denounce evil; no one Truth by which to gauge righteousness. Everything is blurred and blended.

Hear Colson's cryptic words:

> An understanding of truth must precede any conclusions. . . . Otherwise, moral discourse and debate become interminable. "Truth" becomes a matter only of choice or preference. Belief evaporates into mere self-fulfillment, which breeds bizarre alternatives to (biblical) belief.[2]

Another explanation: The media may, simply, be giving people what they demand. According to pollster George Barna, while 97% believe in God, only 67% believe He's the "all-powerful . . . Creator . . . who rules today."[3] Increasingly, He is identified by the nebulous, New Age tag of "higher consciousness."

Combining the two explanations, is there any wonder why Barna discovered that three-quarters of all Americans believe in no absolute truth? Nor, more startling still, why 62% of born-again Christians admit to not believing in it either?![4]

The point is clear: Belief in a personal, holy, just

---

2. Charles Colson, *Christianity Today*, "The Year of the Neopagan," March 6, 1995, p. 88.

3. Ibid.

4. Ibid.

God — One who nurtures, guides as well as judges — is fading fast. Let's examine a few reasons for this unfortunate shift of perspective.

Terminators of a Biblical God-cept

How did so many of us get on this neopagan track?

First, although the numbers of their hard-core adherents are minimal, indeed, the impact of the New Age philosophy has broadsided our American culture. Chuck Colson is right.

Its symbols prevail. Scores wear crystals and chart horoscopes. Celestial paraphernalia even decorate Christmas trees!

Popular literary forms have emerged. Wave music has replaced "elevator tunes" in most shopping centers. Science fiction proclaims New Age themes. Books, like those of high priestess, Shirley McLain (e.g., *Out On A Limb*), have made millions.

Then, there is their whole set of core values, derived from eastern religions, that has afflicted our national psyche. Here is a sampling:

Value	Definition
➤ relativism	There is no absolute truth.
➤ universalism	All belief systems are alike in principle.
➤ pantheism	Nature/universe is god, so man is not unique.
➤ reincarnation	We're all involved in a cycle of rebirths.
➤ mysticism	Only spirit counts; matter is an illusion.

Here is a second factor that has made us

vulnerable: silent parents, who have created a belief vacuum in their offspring.

American parents take great pride in being open in discussing the most intimate and critical issues. But, when children broach the most important question in life — Is there a God? — the sidestepping and back-peddling begins.

It suddenly becomes a game of "dodge ball," using rationalizations as the "ball." Here are a couple of the most common ones:

"Everyone needs to form his own idea about God."
[Why so, if it's not true of other "controversial" subjects (e.g., sex and politics) that we discuss openly?]

"Nobody knows for sure about what He's like."
[If parents only talked about what they were absolutely certain of, dinnertime would be as quiet as a morgue!]

Fact: Studies show that our kids develop their own ideas of God at an early age — even if parents are aloof and evasive. Art Linkletter enjoys telling about the father who, before his kid departed for Sunday School, pinned a note to his shirt that read:

> "The opinions expressed about God, by this child, are not necessarily those of his parents!"

When we communicate embarrassment or distaste, we leave our children adrift — to catch-as-catch-can their God-cept. It's much better for us to employ an informed, creative, intentional and sensitive approach. The key questions become: What ideas about God can we help them to form? Also, how can we best guide, and facilitate, the process?

Let's pursue these three practical suggestions, by David J. Wolpe, for getting ourselves started:

1. *Our culture acknowledges the importance of self-esteem, so why not teach children that they were created in God's image?* Then, no matter whether they succeed or fail, are applauded or rebuked — they'll know to always remind themselves that they are extremely valuable.

2. *For children who feel alone or frightened, what greater source of consolation can top reminding them that the Creator of the universe always knows and cares deeply about them?*

3. *When kids are uncertain how to feel about different kinds of people (abusers, flaky parents, etc.), a gentle reassurance that we're all children of the same eternal Parent can do wonders.*[5]

A spiritual connection to God can dramatically change the lives of children. No need for high pressure fanaticism or constant preaching. Just a kind, intelligent "passing of the baton" to those whose little hands are outstretched.

To abrogate this responsibility, as scores do, is to render our children defenseless in an intrusive, neo-paganistic society.

Supply the Nike™ tennies. Attend the soccer matches. Assist with the science fairs. But, give highest priority to tactfully, and naturally, discussing God.

Why is our God-cept becoming faulty, with all of the accompanying havoc that results? First, we're being assaulted by New Age secularism. Second,

---

5. David J. Wolpe, "Why the Silence About God?" *L.A. Times*, Dec. 19, 1993, p. m-5. (Rabbi Wolpe, author of *Teaching Your Children About God*, Henry Holt and Company, 1993, teaches at the University of Judaism, Los Angeles, CA.)

we're failing to pass on accurate biblical teaching about Him to our children. Allow me to offer just one more reason.

Reality: It's a Ton Stranger Than Fiction!

Finally, as adults claiming to be God's followers, we have bought into distorted and damaging viewpoints of His essential nature.

When asked His identity, God answered: *"I Am That I Am"* (Exod. 3:14). Some have taken that to imply that He is beyond human definition or comprehension. He is the distant "Wholly Other" — never to be known.

At the other extreme, many trivialize Him, by shrinking Him down to handy, manageable size, making God in their image — as a movie star did, when she flippantly described Him as "my living doll."

The truth betrays us: Scores of us have inaccurate ways of thinking about God, and our misconceptions adversely affect our lives. In their book, *Stupid Ways, Smart Ways, To Think About God,* Jack Bemporad and Michael Shevack reveal a plethora of erroneous God descriptors.

Among the "stupid" views of God they list are these:

1. God as personal *"cosmic bellhop,"* who ratifies our every desire, is perpetually ready to serve us, and is eager to help us control others.
2. God as *"little Mary Sunshine,"* who keeps us jubilantly cheerful no matter what goes wrong.
3. God as *"the wrathful Marquis de God,"* who vindictively punishes and exterminates despicable sinners.

4. God as *"our nation's commander-in-chief,"* whose holy mission is to make our country supreme — the leader of our crusades; the general of our jihads.
5. God as the ultimate *"master of ceremonies,"* who can be hired by any of us to officiate at our weddings, bar mitzvahs, confirmations, funerals.

The authors proceed to share "smart" descriptions.

1. God as *"the beginning of the beginning"* of everything — before the big bang, the time-space continuum, energy and matter, and the universe.
2. God as *"living in the present,"* whose infinity and consciousness permeates everything — though He has no need to breathe nor digest food.
3. God as *"Creator,"* the ultimate Prodigy.
4. God as *"Giver to mankind of god-like qualities,"* like free will for "choice," potential for dignity in suffering, intelligence, conscience, and "rope" — enough to climb or "hang ourselves" with.
5. God as *"personal,"* having real consequences for our lives, and presenting us with the standard by which to evaluate our decisions.
6. God as *"forever,"* confronting the power of death, "lifting the executioner's mask" to declare we are immortal — our consciousness lives on.[6]

---

6. Jack Bemporad and Michael Shevack, *L.A. Times,* "Childhood Image of God Prevails Among Adults, Authors Say," n.d. (Rabbi Jack Bemporad and Michael Shevack are co-authors of *Stupid Ways, Smart Ways, to Think about God,* Triumph Books.)

We're indebted for these authors for separating truth from myth, accuracy from falsehood, stepping-stone from stumbling-block. God's essential nature is comprehensible. Furthermore, He will help us to grasp it. For starters, He has presented us with His vitae; we know it as The Bible.

Also, He has generously gifted us with His only Son, who declared to Philip: ". . . *Anyone who has seen me has seen the Father*" (John 14:9).

Finally, His Spirit comes alongside us to gently enlighten our minds and hearts — in a patient, warm and reassuring way. Jesus tells us to constantly remind ourselves: "*He (the Holy Spirit) will guide you into **all** truth*" (John 16:13). In effect, that makes Him our seeing-eye dog, highway map, and Triple-A all wrapped into one!

Well, since the eyes of my heart have been enlightened, and my point of view has been shaped-up, His Spirit has taught me some important lessons about our heavenly Father's nature. And I'm very eager to share.

A Lot More Than A Refresher Course!

First, I learned that He reveals His identity in a way that intercepts us exactly where we are.

He did so to Danny Dutton, age 8, from Chula Vista, California. His third grade teacher asked him to explain "God." Here is what he said:

> One of God's main jobs is making people. He makes these to put in place of the ones that die so there will be enough to take care of things here on earth.
> He doesn't make grownups. Just babies. I think because they are smaller and easier to make. That way he doesn't have to take up His valuable time teaching them to talk and walk. He can just leave that up to the mothers and fathers. I think it works out pretty good.

God's second most important job is listening to prayers. An awful lot of this goes on, as some people, like preachers and things, pray other times beside bedtime. God doesn't have time to listen to the radio or TV on account of this. As He hears everything, not only prayers, there must be a terrible lot of noise going into His ears, unless He has thought of a way to turn it off.

God sees everything and hears everything and is everywhere. Which keeps Him pretty busy. So you shouldn't go wasting His time by going over your parents' head and ask for something they said you couldn't have.

Atheists are people who don't believe in God. I don't think there are any in Chula Vista. At least there aren't any who come to our church.

Jesus is God's Son. He used to do all the hard work like walking on water and doing miracles and trying to teach people about God who didn't want to learn. They finally got tired of Him preaching to them and they crucified Him. But He was good and kind like His Father and He told His Father that they didn't know what they were doing and to forgive them and God said ok. His Dad (God) appreciated everything He had done and all His hard work on earth, so He told Him He didn't have to go out on the road anymore. He could stay in heaven. So He did.

And now He helps His Dad out by listening to prayers and seeing which things are important for God to take care of and which ones He can take care of Himself without having to bother God with. Like a secretary only more important, of course. You can pray anytime you want and they are sure to hear you because they've got it worked out so one of them is on duty all the time.

You should always go to Sunday School because it makes God happy, and if there's anybody you want to make happy, it's God. Don't skip Sunday School to do something you think will be more fun like going to the beach. This is wrong! And besides the sun doesn't come out at the beach until noon, anyway.

If you don't believe in God, besides being an atheist, you will be very lonely, because your parents can't go everywhere with you like to camp, but God can. It's good to know He's around when you're scared of the dark or when you can't swim very good and you get thrown in real deep water by big kids.

But you shouldn't just always think of what God can do for you. I figure God put me here and He can take me back anytime He pleases. And that's why I believe in God.[7]

Humorous? Sure. But the kid is "perspicacious," a term Webster defines as "keenly discerning or understanding — sharp-sighted." Why? Because God met Him right where He was, and revealed crucial truth.

He does that for all of us, if we'll let Him. He has a tailor-made message for each day, each feeling-state we're in, each crisis. And it makes incredible sense — relevant for right where we are on our journey.

Second, His track-record in my life taught me this valuable lesson: When I do my best, He takes care of the rest.

Songwriter Bill Gaither hit the bull's eye when he wrote: "He made something beautiful of my life." That's His style. Isaiah tells us to think of our lives as clay, and Him as our Potter. He tempers, alloys, shapes, molds and polishes. In the prophet's words: "*. . . we all are the work of your hands*" (64:8).

We may see ourselves as nothing, but us plus Him equals an incalculable value. An equation that mathematicians would go crazy trying to figure out!

The best illustration I've come across, of God's added value to our lives, was told by Charles Swindoll. It deeply touched my heart.

Some years ago, Ignace Jan Paderewski, famed composer-pianist, was scheduled to perform at a great American concert hall. It promised to be a memory maker, a high-society extravaganza, with everyone decked-out in black tuxedos and long evening dresses.

---

7. David Davenport read this letter to the Pepperdine University faculty in 1995.

In the audience was a mother with her fidgety nine-year-old son. Tired of waiting, he squirmed restlessly. Why was he there? His mother had hopes that her boy would be encouraged to practice his piano. If only he could hear the immortal Paderewski at the keyboard! So, against his wishes, he was there.

She turned to talk with friends. Her son could stay seated no longer, and slipped away. He was drawn to the ebony concert grand Steinway, flooded with blinding lights.

Without being noticed by the sophisticated audience, the kid plopped down on the stool, and stared wide-eyed at the black and white keys. Then, he placed his small, trembling fingers in the right location and began playing "chopsticks."

The roar of the crowd was hushed. Frowning faces turned in his direction. Irritated, they yelled out:

"Get that boy away from there!"

"Somebody stop him!"

"Where's his mother?"

Backstage, the master overheard the sounds out front, and quickly put together what was happening. Hurriedly, he grabbed his coat and rushed toward the stage. Without a word of announcement, he stooped over the kid, reached around both sides, and began to improvise a countermelody to harmonize with and enhance "chopsticks."

As the two of them played together, Paderewski kept whispering in the boy's ear: "Keep going. Don't quit, son. Keep on playing . . . don't stop."

So it is with us. We strive and struggle, doing our thing. And what we're dedicating ourselves to seems about as significant as "chopsticks." And about the time we're ready to give it up, along comes our Master.

He smiles, leans over us, and whispers: "Now keep going; don't quit. Keep on . . . don't stop; don't quit," as He beautifully improvises on our behalf — adding just the right touch at the right moments.[8]

He's our Booster. Our Potter. Our Encourager. Our #1 Fan. The One who embellishes our thoughts, efforts, goals, dreams — no matter how flawed — if we'll simply not quit trusting and trying!

Cowboy legend, Roy Rogers, used to end his shows with the words: "May the good Lord take a likin' to ya." Well, in reality, He has taken a likin' to all of us! He knows us by name, and even is aware of the number of hairs on our head (Matt. 10:30).

Furthermore, He stands ready to "rush to the stage" the moment we are ready to partner with Him. Result: Something beautiful!

Third, my God is relentless in His pursuit of me — when I run from His presence and will.

One writer describes Him as the "Hound of heaven." The One who relentlessly attempts to track us down, in order to invite us back home. Unfortunately, we often keep running — and keep ignoring His pleas.

By sheer providence, I happened upon this letter. It's from a Friend, and addressed to all of us:

LETTER FROM A FRIEND

I just had to write to tell you how much I love you and care for you. Yesterday, I saw you walking and laughing with your friends; I hoped that soon you'd want Me to walk along with you, too. So, I painted you a sunset to close your day and whispered a cool breeze to refresh you. I waited — you never called — I just kept on loving you.

---

8. Charles R. Swindoll, *Growing Strong in the Seasons Of Life* (Portland: Multnomah Press, 1983), pp. 48-49.

As I watched you fall asleep last night, I wanted so much to touch you. I spilled moonlight onto your face — trickling down your cheeks as so many tears have. You didn't even think of Me; I wanted so much to comfort you.

The next day I exploded a brilliant sunrise into glorious morning for you. But you woke up late and rushed off to work — you didn't even notice. My sky became cloudy and My tears were the rain.

I love you. Oh, if you'd only listen. I really love you. I try to say it in the quiet of the green meadow and in the blue sky. The wind whispers My love through the treetops and spills it into the vibrant colors of the flowers. I shout it to you in the thunder of the great waterfalls and compose love songs for birds to sing to you. I warm you with the clothing of My sunshine and perfume the air with nature's sweet scent.

My love for you is deeper than any ocean and greater than any need in your heart. If you'd only realize how I care.

God[9]

Wes Tracy, in a *Herald of Holiness* editorial, charted the ups and downs of his spiritual journey. In his words: "Every time my own sin or failure created a plunge on the chart, Jesus came after me. He would not let me go."

Furthermore, after he was "caught," there was a fresh outpouring of God's Spirit (*"fountains of refreshment in every thirsty valley"* Ps. 84:5-6 Moffatt), accompanied by renewed vision.[10]

God is, indeed, utterly dependable. Hymnwriter George Matheson is on target in describing Him as the "Love that will not let (us) go."[11] His determina-

---

9. Found in loose-leaf form at Forest Home Christian Conference Center, California. Source unknown.

10. Wesley D. Tracy, *Herald Of Holiness*, "What I Found Out About God, December, 1993, p. 3.

11. George Matheson, "O Love That Will Not Let Me Go" (Isaiah 60:19), *Hymns for the Family of God* (Nashville: Paragon Associates, Incorporated, 1976), p. 404.

tion to save us is stronger than we can ever imagine.

Fourth, I've begun to really understand why God is referred to as "Father."

It seems to be the favorite designation of Jesus, and He entreats His disciples to pray: *"Our Father in heaven . . ."* (Matt. 6:9-13).

This was revolutionary, for they had never conceptualized Him in that manner. The prophets had taught them to see Him as high and lofty, holy and immortal. The Greek philosophers had presented Him in very nebulous, impersonal terms, e.g., the "Unmoved Mover."

Enter Jesus. The One who knows Him best.

In effect, He asks His followers to take all of the best love, of the best fathers, who ever lived. Add it up — and that's only a shadowy hint of the One who called Israel *"the apple of His eye"* (Deut. 32:10)!

Paul picks up on this marvelous imagery, and presents it in full crescendo in this theological symphony:

> For you did not receive a spirit that makes you a slave again to fear, but you received the Spirit of sonship. And by him we cry, 'Abba, Father.' The Spirit himself testifies with our spirit that we are God's children. Now if we are children, then we are heirs — heirs of God and co-heirs with Christ, if indeed we share in his sufferings in order that we may also share in his glory (Rom. 8:15-17).

Not slaves to fear, rather, spiritual sons and heirs — willing to suffer with Him in order to share His glory!

And how about the term, "Abba"? Put simply, it's Hebrew for our word, "Dad da." Informality, warmth, deep affection — they're all implied.

Jesus is telling us to address the infinite, majestic, all-powerful God in baby talk!

What does He have in common with a good father? He loves us as we are, not just as we should be. He uses all our past experiences to bring us where we are now — standing on "holy ground."

And, with Him, we have an easy familiarity. Not a sloppy sentimentality. Not a taken-for-granted, "Man upstairs," over-familiarity. Rather, our familiarity is saturated with a profound reverence and respect.

Brennan Manning advises us to pray each day, with hands upward, "Abba, I belong to you." Its seven syllables correspond with our natural pattern of breathing. And eventually, in his words, we'll "push our head down into our heart."

He advised a nun, who was raped as a child, to follow this practice. It had an incredible effect on her spirit. She later told him, "Brennan, deep down inside, I now feel I'm my 'Daddy's little girl.' And that's made all the difference in the world!"

Manning paraphrases German theologian Joachim Jeremias: God as Abba is the central, primary revelation of Jesus. It opens up an undreamed-of possibility, namely, real intimacy in prayer.

God as Abba gives us an alternative to seeing Him as Policeman with a club, great Hangman in the sky, celestial Ghost, the needling customs Officer — constantly rummaging through our moral suitcase, or distant and unconcerned Supreme Being.

The Abba Father idea gives everything a new climate. Fear and trembling are replaced by faith and trust. John Powell states, "If we really believe that God is our Abba, we should notify our face!"

Worry and fear have no place in His Kingdom!

Some of us can identify with the person who

declared: "I can't stop worrying, if I did, I'd have twelve or fourteen hours a day with nothing to do!" But, not worrying is something we really owe to Him.

And how about fearing Him? It does not compute with the concept of Abba. Manning puts it: "We live in the wisdom of accepted tenderness." He is open, accepting, patient. Allowing us to grow.[12]

Knowing that, we can (to quote Earl Lee) confidently "let ourselves down into His love." And that will cause our striving to relinquish itself to surrender; our fretting to turn into faith.[13]

How about the unanswered questions regarding His nature and actions? Again, the pivotal word is trust. No need to keep asking "why." As Charles Swindoll declares, down deep, we just know that our Abba is:

TOO KIND TO DO ANYTHING CRUEL. . .
TOO WISE TO MAKE A MISTAKE. . .
TOO DEEP TO EXPLAIN HIMSELF. . .[14]

He's our Daddy, and He'll handle everything with our authentic needs and best interests in mind. As the motel commercial states: We'll rest assured!

One parenthetical note: While going through my trial-by-fire, I learned increasingly to warm up to my Abba. And it made all the difference in the world — the biggest one being, now, more than ever before, I'm seeing myself as "my Daddy's little guy."[15]

---

12. Cf. Brennan Manning, *Abba's Child: The Cry of the Heart for Intimate Belonging* (Colorado Springs: NavPress, 1994).

13. Taken from a sermon by Earl Lee, on the subject of "Holiness," heard at Forest Home Christian Conference Center, October, 1995.

14. Swindoll, *Growing Strong*, p. 92.

15. So great was the love between this author and his father,

And how was this realization directly related to cultivating a biblical frame of reference? Let me explain.

Same Song, Different Verse

In Section III, "Growing Strong," we have focused on dividends of allowing God to enlighten the eyes of our hearts. Specifically, we've examined the spill-over effect in life's "wilderness experiences," relationships with others, formulating our self-identity, and fashioning our God-cept.

We've attempted to explain how we can get stuck, in relationship to any (or all) of these. Furthermore, how that stuckness intensely impacts the stuckness we feel when bogged down in relationship impasses.

In my church situation, it had all the earmarks of a bona fide "wilderness." No jackrabbit nor cactus, granted, but as desolate for me as the Sinai desert was for the Israelites.

How did I relate to people? Distrust, near-paranoia, snappiness (even toward those who love me most), withdrawal, and retrenchment began to occur. Around others, I started to feel like a pair of brown shoes on the feet of a guy wearing a black tuxedo! Totally out of place.

Need I explain further about my increasingly depleted self-esteem? A couple of unwanted guests, defensiveness and oversensitivity, crept in.

I began to feel pessimistic, self-doubting and rather useless — especially, to myself.

Leo Johnston, a minister of the Gospel for 48 years, that, as a child, he told anyone who would listen: "I'm my daddy's little guy." Such a relationship with my biological father has facilitated my consideration of God as my spiritual Father.

How about my concept of God? Although I never stopped loving Him, nor believing that He loved me, Satan began to do a number on how I envisioned my heavenly Father.

Providentially, I picked up an article by Christian anthropologist, and former missionary, Joseph Cooke, entitled "I Invented an Impossible God." Not only did it inform me, but jarred me loose.

For starters, he emphatically declares: Whenever we get off track, it's because we lose sight of God's grace. The same conclusion driven home by Steve Green's pastoral message!

He contends that most of us down-home Christians have a fair understanding of basic doctrine. We've passed Head Knowledge 101.

Furthermore, we appreciate God's grace. Only through this marvelous gift are we saved. What's more, at the end of the line, we're assured that His grace will take us through death, the judgment, and onward to our heavenly reward.

But, according to Cooke, it's in our daily living — the time-gap between being saved and reaching the end — that our perspective of God is graceless. "Life is one long, deadly grind of trying to be perfect to earn the daily pleasure of a God who simply (cannot) be pleased."[16]

According to this point of view, His demands are so high and His opinion of us is so low, that we can only frown and keep on "scrubbing (ourselves) in His bathtub."

Another characteristic of our non-gracious God is His nagging. He's constantly after us to do this and

---

16. Joseph Cooke, *Eternity Magazine*, "I Invented An Impossible God, May, 1978, pp. 37-39.

not do that. Pray more. Spend more time reading the Bible. No more wicked thoughts. Yield! Confess! Work harder.

No matter how hard we try, with this point of view, it's never ever quite good enough. And before long, we're unable to differentiate between His loving rebuke (for our benefit) and scathing accusation (for our condemnation).

Still another characteristic of our fictitious ungracious God: He continuously shows us the nail-pierced Hands of our Savior, reminding us of the cost of redemption. In so doing, His love becomes a weapon to compel us to do things we don't really have in our heart to do.

Grace becomes a kind of nongrace. We feel ashamed and guilty. Like Adam and Eve in the Garden, we can only look around for a place to hide!

A final characteristic: This ungracious God, bottom line, considers us less than dirt! Sure, He sent His Son to die, and even referred to us as the "apple of His eye." But, once again, that pertains to the beginning and end — not these in-between times.

Then comes this rider: We feel that His day-by-day love and acceptance is conditioned on our inviting Him to crush nearly everything that is "us." To squelch our personhood. To create a righteous phantom. To extinguish self-worth, and be brought down to zero — so that He is able to, according to Cooke, "pull the strings of our life and make us into a marionette, dancing to the will of our divine Puppeteer."

Why do we tolerate living with such an ungracious God? In addition to making our life miserable, we're ignoring His authentic Persona — as carefully delineated in His Word!

How can we escape this incredibly mistaken point of view? The author provides these tips. Tips that can help us breathe freely again:

1. **Refrain from reading the Bible or praying again until we really want to.** That is sure to kill the "dutiful religion" bit.

2. **Learn to be stubborn.** Let's refuse to be pushed around by those toxic expectations of ourselves and others, or even by what a diseased conscience tells us God expects.

3. **Go beyond such stubbornness and learn to accept God's unconditional acceptance.** This means believing that He accepts us as we are, and accepting ourselves in the same way — our inadequacies, hopes, fears.

4. **Make peace with emotions.** Rather than fighting or burying them, we must understand and express them freely before our accepting Father — just like the Psalmist, Job and Jesus (in the Garden of Gethsemane) did.

5. **Affirm sonship.** "(That means) repudiating (our) doormat stance, (our) worm-like theology, (our) false meekness, (our) passive compliance." That means rejoicing in what God made, when He sculpted us! Also, it implies taking responsibility for using our minds and hearts to make choices that please Him — not remaining a "passive puppet," that expects Him to decide everything.[17]

In the deepest corner of our heart-of-hearts, we know that these lessons can do wonders for us. Key point: we must be patient with ourselves, realizing that it takes time to reprogram entrenched habits and

---

17. Ibid.

mindsets. To change lenses on the eyes of our heart.

Nevertheless, we can be assured that He promises to help us restructure our entire life on the basis of His grace principle. So that our perceptions, reactions, attitudes, feelings, decisions, servanthood, habits and relationships are impacted by His loving Lordship.

It's time we squared away our vision of God. It's guaranteed to do wonders for our lives.

Some Crucial Questions to Ponder

1. What atheistic, or neopagan (e.g., New Age) influences have I run across? Have I responded in ways that, I feel, would please God?

2. What was the predominant God-cept of my childhood? Was it like Danny Dutton's? To what extent was it accurate? How is it compared with the way(s) I envision Him today?

3. Did I ever have a "Paderewski" experience, with God behind me saying: "Keep going. Don't quit." What were my thoughts and feelings then and, as I look back upon it, now?

4. Do I really, truly believe that God is my Father? Do my thoughts, attitudes and behavior testify to this belief?

Concluding Remarks

Seen a garnet lately? It's the richly-hued birth-stone of persons, like my mother, born in January.

Here's something else: This reddish-brown gem-stone has great historical significance. Ancient kings made it the centerpiece of their treasured breast-plate. And tradition has it that Noah placed one on the bow of his ark!

What is so special about the garnet?

It was believed that all stones on earth merely reflect light — except for one, the garnet. It alone generates illumination from within. And for that rea-son, it was commonly referred to as the "third eye."

Before the days of electricity, the garnet was cov-eted for times of emergency. When all was pitch dark, people thought that it would beam forth its inner light.

Today's scientists scoff at such superstition, but the garnet's symbolism is too striking to ignore. It offers a great lesson for our lives.

Most people around us are, simply, reflectors. Treated nicely, they respond with smiles and gracious words. Guaranteed.

But, dealt a bit of opposition or hardship, they're

likely to "go ballistic" — indulging in such things as self-pity, resentment, denial and aggressiveness. For me, it was all of the above!

Before God helped me to begin "seeing" my situation with spiritually-enlightened eyes, I merely reflected back the negative I had received. Feeling misperceived, misjudged and mistreated, I allowed myself to get off track. Evidence?

➤ I nagged God, demanding answers to two questions: *"Why?"* and *"Why me?"*

➤ For the one whose vision of me was so distorted, I wished for retribution.

➤ Worst of all, I actually thought that my rightness, cleverness or sincerity, alone, would cause everything to correct itself.

A garnet I wasn't. More like a gray millstone, sliding into the depths of the sea! What was the source of my difficulty? Plain and simple, I *sought light from an external source rather than an internal Force.*

How did I start to become victorious over my predicament?

Put simply, I asked God to enlighten the eyes of my heart. Just as He did for persons described in His Word.

Most biblical heroes encountered folks who tried to do them in, even though they only desired to serve God and live in peace.

In the Old Testament, Moses had his Pharaoh, Abel his Cain, Joseph his brothers, David his Saul, Samuel his sons, Job his accusers.

Likewise, the New Testament tells how Peter had his Sanhedrin, Stephen his stone-throwers, and Paul his Demetrius.

These saints weren't made of Teflon; they felt pain

deeply. Nevertheless, they emerged triumphant. Why? Because their perspective was truly spiritual. Their eyes were focused on things eternal. Their trust was in God alone.

I needed, and deeply desired, what they had.

Call it what you will. Paradigm-shift. Reframing. A brand new point of view. I desperately needed a thoroughly Christian way of seeing life. One that would help me to not be traumatized by persecution. One that would assure me of coping, regardless of circumstances.

Just like the blind man along Palestine's dusty road, two millennia ago, Jesus touched my eyes. With Him, I've started climbing "Mount Perspective" — where the air is crisp and clear, and the vision is spectacular!

As a result, my life isn't — and can never be — the same!

Appendixes

Appendixes

Personal Strengths Survey

How to take it:

In this survey, you need only circle a few words that describe yourself. With that information, you will be shown your unique strengths and why they make you such a valuable person in all your relationships.

To complete the instrument, just read through the four boxes below (the L, B, O, and G boxes), and circle each word or phrase that seems to describe a consistent character trait of yours. Next, add the number of words and phrases you circled in each box. Then there's only one more step: you double your score to come up with a total in each box.

If that's all the instruction you need, go ahead and take the survey. But, if you're the type of person who thinks these things should be more complicated, here are some additional details.

As you'll notice, each box has fourteen words or word groups (like "Takes charge," "determined" and "firm") and one phrase (like "Let's do it now!").

In the first box (with an L above it), you might read each word or phrase and decide to circle only one word as representing a fairly consistent character trait of yours. On the other hand, you might decide that all fourteen words and even the phrase apply to you. In that case, you would end up with all fifteen choices circled.

Go through each box, circling as many words and phrases as describe who you are consistently. Then double the number of words you circled to come up with a total score for each.

Remember that if you don't circle at least one word or phrase in one of the four boxes, you probably don't have a personality!

Finally, take the total scores from all the boxes and transfer them to the graph below the survey. The last thing left is something that most of us enjoy doing: connect the dots.

As you take this short self-survey, keep two things in mind. First, circle your responses based on how you relate to the people in your family — the most important people in your life. However, you may also want to make a copy of this inventory and take it again based on how you respond to people in another setting, e.g., work, school, etc. Why?

Many people tend to shift their actions and attitudes between home and other settings. We've seen many men, for example, who are extremely hardside at work, but who are out of balance softside at home. This inconsistency can cause much personal stress.

Second, be sure to circle responses based on who you actually are and how you act toward others right now — not on how you wish you were or always wanted to be. Can you make yourself look "better" than you really are on this survey? Certainly. Should you? Not if you want an honest evaluation of who you are and how you relate to others. That's one reason we ask people to have a loved one or close friend fill out the survey based on how they see them; it's a way to get a more objective analysis.

THE PERSONAL STRENGTHS SURVEY

Once again, in each box, circle each word or phrase that describes a consistent character trait of yours. Total the number circled in each box, then double your score. Take a few minutes now to complete the survey and fill in the graph which follows.

L		B	
Takes charge	Bold	Deliberate	Discerning
Determined	Purposeful	Controlled	Detailed
Assertive	Decision maker	Reserved	Analytical
Firm	Leader	Predictable	Inquisitive
Enterprising	Goal driven	Practical	Precise
Competitive	Self-reliant	Orderly	Persistent
Enjoys Challenges	Adventurous	Factual	Scheduled
"Let's do it now!"		*"How was that done in the past?"*	
Double the number circled		**Double the number circled**	
O		G	
Takes risks	Fun-loving	Loyal	Adaptable
Visionary	Likes variety	Nondemanding	Sympathetic
Motivator	Enjoys change	Even keel	Thoughtful
Energetic	Creative	Avoids conflict	Nurturing
Very verbal	Group oriented	Enjoys routine	Patient
Promoter	Mixes easily	Dislikes change	Tolerant
Avoids details	Optimistic	Deep relationships	Good listener
"Trust me! It'll work out!"		*"Let's keep things the way they are"*	
Double the number circled		**Double the number circled**	

The Personal Strengths Survey Chart

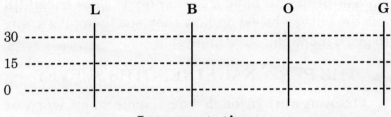

Interpretation

After you've taken the instrument and transferred your scores to the chart, what does it all mean?

The four letters at the top of each section stand for the four basic personality types described in the text. Whether we tend to be hard or soft in relationships. As you'll see everyone is a combination of all four of these types. But for now, let's take a quick overview of the four animals.

Scoring high on the **L** line are those we call **lions**. Lions are take-charge leaders. They're usually the bosses at work, or at least they think they are! They're decisive, bottom-line folks who are doers, not watchers or listeners. They love to solve problems. Unfortunately, however, if they don't learn to use both sides of love, their natural hardside bent can cause problems with others.

Scoring high on the **B** line are those we call **beavers**. Beavers have a strong need to do things "right" and "by the book." In fact, they're the kind of people who actually read instruction manuals! They like maps, charts and organization. And they're great at providing quality control for a home or office.

Because rules, consistency and high standards are so important to beavers, they often communicate the hard side of love to others just like lions. Beavers have deep feelings for those they love. But learning to balance the two sides of love usually involves adding the ability to communicate that softness and warmth in a way that's felt and clearly understood by others.

Scoring high on the **O** line are the **otters**. Otters are excitable, fun-seeking cheerleader types who love to yak. They're great at motivating others and need to be in an environment where they get to talk and have a vote on major decisions.

Otters' outgoing nature makes them great networkers — they usually know people who know people who know people. The only problem is, they usually don't know everyone's name! They can be very soft and encouraging with others (unless under pressure, when they tend to use their verbal skills to attack). But because of their strong desire to be liked, they can often fail to be hard on problems and cause further problems as a result.

Scoring high on the **G** line are the **golden retrievers**. These people are just like their counterparts in nature. If you could pick one word to describe them, it would be "loyalty." They're so loyal, in fact, that they can absorb the most emotional pain and punishment in relationships — and still stay committed. They're great listeners, empathizers and warm encouragers — all strong softside skills. But they tend to be such pleasers that they can have great difficulty in adding the hard side of love when it's needed.

Instrument Number Two

FINDING YOUR PERSONAL BALANCE POINT

How to take it (example):

Takes the lead   Follower

1	2	3	4	5	6	7

If you tend to take the lead in your relationships quickly and consistently, you would circle 1. If you tend to follow the other person's directions or wishes the majority of the time, you would circle 7. If you fall somewhere between these two extremes, you would circle whatever number best represents how you relate to your loved one.

A hardside/softside evaluation

How do you tend to act in your relationship with _____ ? (Loved one)

1. Take the lead   Follower

1   2   3   4   5   6   7

2. Forceful   Nondemanding

1   2   3   4   5   6   7

3. Energetic   Reserved

1   2   3   4   5   6   7

4. Strive to accomplish personal goals   Let others set your goals

1   2   3   4   5   6   7

5. Be self-controlled   Lack discipline

1   2   3   4   5   6   7

6. Make quick decisions   Hesitate in making decisions

1   2   3   4   5   6   7

7. Want to hear facts   Want to share feelings

1   2   3   4   5   6   7

8. A motivator   Responder

1   2   3   4   5   6   7

9. Highly competitive   Noncompetitive
1   2   3   4   5   6   7

10. Possessive   Sharing
1   2   3   4   5   6   7

11. Assertive   Shy
1   2   3   4   5   6   7

12. Express anger to others   Hold anger inside
1   2   3   4   5   6   7

13. Resist correction   Very teachable
1   2   3   4   5   6   7

14. Share your opinions openly   Hide your true feelings
1   2   3   4   5   6   7

15. Function well under pressure   Function poorly
1   2   3   4   5   6   7

16. Lecture when the person   Listen and comfort
      is hurting
1   2   3   4   5   6   7

17. Hold grudges   Forgive easily
1   2   3   4   5   6   7

18. Set rigid standards   Set flexible standards
1   2   3   4   5   6   7

19. Hard on him/her as a person   Soft on him/her
1   2   3   4   5   6   7

20. Hard on his/her problems   Soft on his/her problems
1   2   3   4   5   6   7

Scoring:

Total of all the numbers circled = _____
Mark your total score with an "X" on the line below.

Intensity Index

Hardside   Softside

| 20 | 40 | 60 | 80 | 100 | 120 | 140 |

Interpretation

Many people find themselves scoring in the 75 to 105 range. This often indicates an ability to give and take in expressing the two sides of love. Those scoring below 65 or above 115 typically express one side much more than the other.

Remember that your score should be cross-checked by a loved one or close friend to see how the person views you. We've often seen people score themselves in the middle of the scale, while loved ones place them at one of the extremes.[1]

---

1. Taken from Gary Smalley and John Trent, Ph.D., *The Two Sides of Love: What Stregthens Affection, Closeness and Lasting Commitment?* (Pomona, CA: Focus on the Family Publishing), pp. 32-36, 21-25. Copyright © 1990, 1992. Used by permission of Focus on the Family.

Explanatory Style Inventory

Instructions: For each question, please circle the one response that you most agree with.

1. If my bank's monthly checking account statement arrived, and its total was $12.63 less than the total in my checkbook, I'd assume it was my (not their) mistake. [A]

    1 for certain   4 probably not
    2 probably   5 not a chance
    3 maybe or maybe not

2. When I have an argument with someone, down deep I am quite certain that bad feelings between us will last for a long time. [B]

    1 for certain   4 probably not
    2 probably   5 not a chance
    3 maybe or maybe not

3. Some days don't go well at all. When this happens to me, I let people around me know about my frustration. [C]

    1 for certain   4 probably not
    2 probably   5 not a chance
    3 maybe or maybe not

4. I'm one of those people who feels bad for a long time after being criticized. [B]

    1 for certain   4 probably not

    2 probably   5 not a chance

    3 maybe or maybe not

5. When I say the wrong thing, I get very embarrassed. [A]

    1 for certain   4 probably not

    2 probably   5 not a chance

    3 maybe or maybe not

6. If I were in a car wreck, it would bring significant stress to those closest to me. [C]

    1 for certain   4 probably not

    2 probably   5 not a chance

    3 maybe or maybe not

7. When people whisper I feel they are talking about me. [A]

    1 for certain   4 probably not

    2 probably   5 not a chance

    3 maybe or maybe not

8. If I received bad news from a friend, about the results of his cancer tests, it would depress me for a long time. [B]

    1 for certain   4 probably not

    2 probably   5 not a chance

    3 maybe or maybe not

9. On days when I think my appearance isn't at its best, (e.g., "bad hair day"), I feel people are looking at me in a negative way. [C]

    1 for certain   4 probably not

    2 probably   5 not a chance

    3 maybe or maybe not

10. If I were to lose my job, I'd be very insecure about finding an acceptable new one. [B]
    1 for certain   4 probably not
    2 probably   5 not a chance
    3 maybe or maybe not

11. When someone fails to follow my instructions, I assume that I didn't explain clearly enough. [A]
    1 for certain   4 probably not
    2 probably   5 not a chance
    3 maybe or maybe not

12. When I fail, I hurt those who care most about me. [C]
    1 for certain   4 probably not
    2 probably   5 not a chance
    3 maybe or maybe not

13. When something I'm using breaks, my first reaction is to assume it was my fault. [A]
    1 for certain   4 probably not
    2 probably   5 not a chance
    3 maybe or maybe not

14. Troubles and problems seem to stay around for a long time. [B]
    1 for certain   4 probably not
    2 probably   5 not a chance
    3 maybe or maybe not

15. If I fail, or let down, people around me suffer or are seriously inconvenienced. [C]
    1 for certain   4 probably not
    2 probably   5 not a chance
    3 maybe or maybe not

16. When I am at a party, and others do not talk to me, I assume it is because I'm not seen as a desirable

person to converse with. [A]

    1 for certain   4 probably not
    2 probably   5 not a chance
    3 maybe or maybe not

17. If I found out that a friend of mine said something bad about me, I know that it could never be the same between us. [B]

    1 for certain   4 probably not
    2 probably   5 not a chance
    3 maybe or maybe not

18. If I forgot to bring donuts to my class, on a day I had promised to do so, I'd feel that most everyone in the class would think badly of me. [C]

    1 for certain   4 probably not
    2 probably   5 not a chance
    3 maybe or maybe not

19. Should the IRS notify me that I was getting audited, I'd blame myself for not making sure that I (or my accountant) had done a good job on the tax return. [A]

    1 for certain   4 probably not
    2 probably   5 not a chance
    3 maybe or maybe not

20. If I had run out of paid "sick days," and had to miss work for a week, I'd know that my finances would be adversely affected for a long time. [B]

    1 for certain   4 probably not
    2 probably   5 not a chance
    3 maybe or maybe not

21. If at a grocery store checkout line, and I had something that needed to be priced by a clerk, I'd feel that all the people were frustrated with me because

of the delay. [C]

    1 for certain   4 probably not

    2 probably   5 not a chance

    3 maybe or maybe not

22. When asked a question in front of others, I hesitate to answer — even if I'm pretty sure of the answer — because I'm afraid of the reactions if I'm wrong. [A]

    1 for certain   4 probably not

    2 probably   5 not a chance

    3 maybe or maybe not

23. If my boss spoke to me in an unkind manner, I would know that this is only the beginning of something worse to come. [B]

    1 for certain   4 probably not

    2 probably   5 not a chance

    3 maybe or maybe not

24. At a restaurant, if I were with a group being served, and my steak were not cooked sufficiently, so that I had to send it back, I'd feel that the group, as well as the waiter, would be upset with me. [C]

    1 for certain   4 probably not

    2 probably   5 not a chance

    3 maybe or maybe not

25. On the way to an important meeting, if I realized that I forgot an important document, I'd blame myself alone — not my tight schedule, persons who didn't remind me, etc. [A]

    1 for certain   4 probably not

    2 probably   5 not a chance

    3 maybe or maybe not

26. If I started on a diet, then stopped, if I ever

started again — down deep — I'd know that I would probably fail again. [B]

1 for certain   4 probably not
2 probably   5 not a chance
3 maybe or maybe not

27. If I had a part in a pageant (play) at church, and I forgot my lines, I'd know that everyone there would be making fun of me. [C]

1 for certain   4 probably not
2 probably   5 not a chance
3 maybe or maybe not

28. If I'm late to an appointment, bottom line, it is my fault — regardless of what delayed me. [A]

1 for certain   4 probably not
2 probably   5 not a chance
3 maybe or maybe not

29. If I were involved in a car accident, and had to rent a car, I'd know to expect long-term complications and inconveniences. [B]

1 for certain   4 probably not
2 probably   5 not a chance
3 maybe or maybe not

30. A relative living close becomes ill. I am unable to respond as I would have liked, due to other commitments. Result: I just know that my other relatives are likely to be critical of me. [C][1]

1 for certain   4 probably not
2 probably   5 not a chance
3 maybe or maybe not

---

1. Based on Martin Seligman's *"optimism-pessimism"* data, the letters in square brackets correspond with his three dimensions: [A] = internal vs. external; [B] = stable vs. unstable; [C] = global vs. specific. See chapter 8 for an explanation of each of these.

Scoring: Please notice that each response has a number. Total the numbers of the responses you circled. Then, match your overall total with the categories below to see how "optimistic" or "pessimistic" your explanatory style is.

My total is _____
This places me in this category _____

Score	Category
30-45	strong pessimistic tendency
46-75	moderate pessimistic tendency
76-105	unclear tendency
106-135	moderate optimistic tendency
136-150	strong optimistic tendency

My reaction to the result revealed by this inventory is:

Four American Generations
(Their parenting style and principal values)

1. Key Principles:
   A. The way I see the world is a result of the world I have seen.
   B. Therefore, I can only motivate people through their own value system, not mine. (I.e., motivational structures are a result of one's value system.)
2. Four Historical Eras:
   A. 1914-1921 (World War I)

   Attitude: Hard work, commitment, diligence

   Childrearing: Child's erotic impulses are dangerous, and should be controlled. (learn respect for authority)

   Principal Values:
   1) patriotic
   2) children are merely little adults
   3) strict attitudes toward sex, nudity and sensuality (e.g., bind male in bed, so he will not touch his genitals)
   B. 1922-1928 (Prohibition)

   Attitude: Be patient. If you work hard all your life, you will get everything you want or deserve.

Childrearing: Childcare varies, depending on who your parents were, and where you were born

Principal Values:

Period of social contradictions (e.g., prohibition, but also the "flapper era"

C. 1929-1941 (Depression Years)

Attitude: Though worked hard, things didn't turn out as they had hoped.

Childrearing: Bowel training must be carried out as early as possible (with severity). Children should be trained not heard, for they must not win out in the struggle for domination. Wean child late, but instantaneously.

Principal Values:

1) Life is a series of tasks to be trained for.
2) Value systems are formed in work characterized by harshness, uncertainty, deprivation, instability and economic insecurity.
3) Know the true meaning of a dollar, and work for it.
4) Reminisce on the past, but vow never to live like that again (i.e., economic need). (Wanted children to have affluence, comfort, ease, technology and education.)

D. 1942-1947 (World War II)

Attitude: It's time to attain things we never had.

Childrearing: Child is less dangerous as an erotic being; he just needs to explore. He needs attention and care upon demand. (Childrearing advice: child rearing became childcare.)

Principal Values:

1) Live in extended families and in communities where people know one another.
2) Possess a "deprivation consciousness" (i.e., remember when times were tough), but be optimistic about the future.
3) Large families are good. Led to baby boom.

Note: After these periods came the "post-war period." It is characterized by the following.

❖ Nuclear family isolation

❖ Absent father (fathers far from home)

❖ Families moved to suburbs

❖ Geographical mobility

❖ Social consciousness

❖ Invention of TV: created "TV generation"

Summary of Conflicting Cultural Assumptions and Values*

American
(Western, urban)

Contrast-American
(Eastern, Third World, rural/tribal)

1. Definition of Activity

a. How do people approach activity?

| (1) Concern with doing, progress, change | Being Spontaneous expressions |
| (2) Optimistic, achievement | Fatalistic |

b. What is the desirable pace of life?

| (1) Fast, busy | Steady, rhythmic |
| (2) Driving | Noncompulsive |

c. How important are goals in planning?

| (1) Stresses means, procedures, techniques | Stresses final goals |

d. What are important goals of life?

(1) Material goals	Spiritual goals
(2) Comfort and absence of pain	Fullness of pleasure and pain
(3) Activity	Experience

e. Where does the responsibility for decisions lie?

| (1) Each individual | Function of a group or resides in a role |

f. At what level do people live?

| (1) Operational, goals evaluated in terms of consequence | Experimental truth |

g. On what basis do people evaluate?

| (1) Utility (does it work?) | Essence (ideal) |

h. Who should make decisions?

| (1) The people affected | Those with proper authority |

"American"   **"Contrast-American"**

i. What is the nature of problem solving?

    (1) Planning behavior   Coping behavior

    (2) Anticipates consequences   Classifies the situation

j. What is the nature of learning?

    (1) Learner is active   Learner is passive

       (student-centered learning) (serial, rote learning)

2. Definition of Social Relations

a. How are roles defined?

    (1) Attained   Ascribed

    (2) Loosely   Tightly

    (3) Generally   Specifically

b. How do people relate to others whose status is different?

    (1) Stresses equality;   Stresses hierarchical ranks; stresses

       minimizes differences   differences, especially to superiors

    (2) Stresses informality   Stresses formality; behavior more

       and spontaneity   easily anticipated

c. How are sex roles defined?

    (1) Similar, overlapping   Distinct

    (2) Sex equality   Male superiority

    (3) Friends of both sexes   Friends of same sex only

    (4) Less legitimized   Legitimized

d. What are members' rights and duties in a group?

    (1) Assumes limited liability Assumes unlimited liability

    (2) Joins group to seek own Accepts constraints by group

       goals

    (3) Active members can   Leader runs group; members do not

       influence

e. How do people judge others?

    (1) Specific abilities or interests Overall individuality of person

                         & his status

    (2) Task-centered   Person-centered

    (3) Fragmentary involvement Total involvement

f. What is the meaning of friendship?

    (1) Social friendship (short Intense friendship (long commit-

       commitment, friends   ment, friends are exclusive)

       shared)

g. What is the nature of social reciprocity?

    (1) Real only   Ideal and real

    (2) Nonbinding (Dutch treat) Binding

    (3) Equal (Dutch treat)   Unequal

h. How do people regard friendly aggression in social interaction?

    (1) Acceptable, interesting, fun Not acceptable, embarrassing

"American"	"Contrast-American"

3. Motivation

a. What is the motivating force?

    (1) Achievement   Ascription

b. How is the person-person competition evaluated?

    (1) As constructive, healthy   As destructive, antisocial

4. Perception of the World (Worldview)

a. What is the (natural) world like?

(1) Physical	Spiritual
(2) Mechanical	Organic
(3) Use of machines	Disuse of machines

b. How does the world operate?

(1) In a rational, learnable manner	In a mystically ordered, spiritually conceived manner (fate)
(2) Chance and probability	No chance nor probability

c. What is the nature of man?

(1) Apart from nature or from any hierarchy	Part of nature or of some hierarchy
(2) Impermanent, not fixed, changeable	Permanent, fixed, not changeable

d. What is the relationship between man and nature?

(1) Good is unlimited	Good is limited
(2) Man should modify nature for his ends	Man should accept the natural order
(3) Good health and material comforts are expected and desired	Some disease and material misery are natural, to be expected

e. What is the nature of truth? goodness?

(1) Tentative (working type)	Definite
(2) Relative to circumstances	Absolute
(3) Experience analyzed in separate components; dichotomies	Experience apprehended as a whole

f. How is time defined? valued?

(1) Future (anticipated)	Past (remembrance) or present experience
(2) Precise units	Undifferentiated
(3) Limited resource	Not limited (not resource)
(4) Lineal	Circular, undifferentiated

g. What is the nature of property?

(1) Private ownership important as extension of self	Use of "natural" purpose regardless of ownership

"American"   "Contrast-American"

5. Perception of the Self and the Individual

a. In what sorts of terms is self defined?
- (1) Diffuse, changing terms   Fixed, clearly defined terms
- (2) Flexible behavior   Person is located in a social system

b. Where does a person's identity seem to be?
- (1) Within the self   Outside the self in roles, groups,
  (achievement)   family, clan, caste, society

c. What is the nature of the individual?
- (1) Separate aspects (intent, Totality of person
  thought, act, biographical
  background

d. On whom should a person place reliance?
- (1) Self   Status, superiors, patron, others
- (2) Impersonal organizations   Persons

e. What kind of person is valued and respected?
- (1) Youthful (vigorous)   Aged (wise, experienced)

f. What is the basis of social control?
- (1) Persuasion, appeal to the Formal, authoritative
  individual

*David S. Hoopes and Paul Ventura, eds., *Intercultural Source Book* (Chicago: Intercultural Press, 1979), pp. 48-51.

Jesus: Name Above All Names*

In GENESIS Jesus is the Ram at Abraham's altar

In EXODUS He's the Passover Lamb

In LEVITICUS He's the High Priest

In NUMBERS He's the Cloud by day and the Pillar of fire by night

In DEUTERONOMY He's the City of our refuge

In JOSHUA He's the scarlet Thread out Rahab's window

In JUDGES He is our Judge

In RUTH He is our Kinsman Redeemer

In 1ST & 2ND SAMUEL He's our Trusted Prophet

And in KINGS and CHRONICLES He's our Reigning King

In EZRA He is our Faithful Scribe

In NEHEMIAH He's the Rebuilder of everything that is broken

And in ESTHER He is the Mordecai sitting faithful at the gate

In JOB He's our Redeemer that ever liveth

In PSALMS He is my Shepherd and I shall not want

In PROVERBS and ECCLESIASTES He's our Wisdom

And in the SONG OF SOLOMON He's the Beautiful Bridegroom

In ISAIAH He's the Suffering Servant

In JEREMIAH and LAMENTATIONS it is Jesus that is the Weeping Prophet

In EZEKIEL He's the the Wonderful Four-Faced Man

And in DANIEL He is the Fourth Man in the midst of a fiery furnace

In HOSEA He is my Love that is forever faithful

In JOEL He baptizes us with the Holy Spirit

In AMOS He's our Burden Bearer

In OBADIAH our Savior

And in JONAH He is the Great Foreign Missionary that takes the Word of God into all the world

You go on and see in MICAH He is the Messenger with beautiful feet

In NAHUM He is the Avenger

In HABAKKUK He is the Watchman that is ever praying for revival

In ZEPHANIAH He is the Lord mighty to save

In HAGGAI He is the Restorer of our lost heritage

In ZECHARIAH He is our Fountain

And in MALACHI He is the Son of Righteousness with healing in His wings

In MATTHEW Thou art the Christ, the Son of the Living God

In MARK He is the Miracle Worker

In LUKE He is the Son of Man

And in JOHN He is the Door by which everyone of us must enter

In ACTS He is the Shining Light that appears to Saul on the road to Damascus

In ROMANS He is our Justifier

In 1st CORINTHIANS our Resurrection

In 2nd CORINTHIANS our Sin Bearer

In GALATIANS He redeems us from the law

In EPHESIANS He is our Unsearchable Riches

In PHILIPPIANS He supplies our every need

And in COLOSSIANS He's the Fullness of the Godhead Bodily

In 1st & 2nd THESSALONIANS He is our Soon Coming King

In 1st & 2nd TIMOTHY He is the Mediator between God

and man

In TITUS He is our Blessed Hope

In PHILEMON He is a Friend that sticks closer than a brother

And in HEBREWS He's the Blood of the everlasting covenant

In JAMES it is the Lord that heals the sick

In 1ST & 2ND PETER He is the Chief Shepherd

In 1ST, 2ND & 3RD JOHN it is Jesus who has the tenderness of love

In JUDE He is the Lord coming with 10,000 saints

And in REVELATION, lift up your eyes, Church, for your redemption draweth nigh, He is the King of kings and Lord of lords!

---

*J.B. Chapman, for a sermon at the General Assembly of the Church of the Nazarene. Date unknown.

Name and Subject Index

Scripture Index